ACTIVATE
YOUR
PASSION

CREATE
YOUR
CAREER

ISBN: 0692270914
ISBN-13: 978-0692270912

Mom & Dad—your support is unsurpassed.
To all others who have contributed to my life and
this project—thank you.

CONTENTS

INTRODUCTION

People are my passion. Not the property, the people The place where sunlight slants through a window onto a hardwood floor is a house. The place where a child lies on that floor with his dog and watches the dust motes drift through that sunlight is a home. If you remove the people and their belongings, the house will slowly deteriorate and crumble into the earth. It's the people that keep the home alive.

As a child, I loved spending time with all sorts of people. It was a quest to connect with others—my teachers, my grandparents, other adults, babies, my peers—it really didn't matter. At that age, I didn't understand the correlation between the connection with people and my own happiness. That would not come until much later. Once it did, though, once I recognized the idea that people were my passion, something exciting happened. Something energizing; something that would give me a new sense of direction and a clear path toward the success that I craved—that we all crave. I learned how to channel my passion for people into a fulfilling career. That is what this book is about: recognizing your passion and channeling it into your own successful career. I can assure you that my rapid escalation in this ultracompetitive industry didn't blossom because I possessed secret strategies, but rather because I recognized my passion and took action.

My name is Madison Hildebrand. I am thirty-three years old. Since entering the real estate industry nine years ago, I've sold over $250 million worth of property. I've been recognized as one of the top producing agents in my area. My company has awarded me with plaques and fancy titles; and really, who doesn't enjoy receiving plaques and fancy titles? It has been tremendously exciting. *Every day* remains tremendously exciting! All of this became possible the moment I activated my passion.

You might think that I am just lucky, but success has very little to do with luck. It has everything to do with passion, attitude, goals, and good old-fashioned hard work. It is about taking action, regardless of your fears.

So much of my success can be attributed to finding and activating my passion for people. Frankly, real estate is the career that presented itself as the most feasible and opportune career path I could take toward living in my passion. Working with people could have resulted in hundreds of career choices.

After graduating college I struggled with what I was going to do next, as do so many people. My father's voice—a stern, trusting one—urged me to work for Corporate America, while part of me longed for an advertising career. However, my job during the last two years of college was at a hotel, which made me believe it was the hotel industry for which I was best suited.

Becoming a realtor was never part of my life plan. I went to Pepperdine University to study advertising. I graduated with a degree in what I thought was my passion. *Advertising* was part of my plan, not *real estate*. Then again, many aspects of my life have taken me by surprise, never having been part of my childhood dreams or my adolescent plans. I came to the real estate business as a very young man. There were three hundred other agents working in Malibu, a town of only fourteen thousand people. I was fresh out of college, with limited business experience and little money saved. I knew very little about real estate. However, I *believed* it was possible and I refused to define failure. To me, it was an opportunity to be happy, to interact with people—*my passion*—during the very intimate process of choosing and purchasing a home.

This book shares my experiences from the first years of my real estate career and the life that informs that career. The suggestions, tools, and stories in this book are applicable to most careers. I have gained some incredible tools; tangible tools that I believe will help you succeed in your career. Had I known earlier what I have written in this book, I could have been even more successful.

Continue to read with an open mind. Reflect upon yourself and decide how you will activate your passion.

Remember, the recommendations in this book are merely suggestions. They work together to create a synergy and a formula for success, regardless of your industry. Ultimately, you will need to find your own path, as I found mine. I wrote this book with the simple intention of sharing intimate details from my journey in hopes of helping others with theirs.

CHAPTER 1

Find Your Passion

As a child, I moved countless times with my family. We lived in nine homes in seven cities across five states before I attended college. I am the middle child of three brothers. My parents, still happily married, recently retired from careers in Corporate America.

Our first big move was from San Diego, California, to Dallas, Texas. I was leaving a community in which I was very involved. I had a lot of friends, I played sports, I knew the ins and outs of my neighborhood, and it was comfortable.

However, my dad accepted a new position, which brought us to Dallas. I experienced a tremendous culture shock! I was the new kid. I knew no one. That move led to a lonely and difficult time. Sure, a new house and new community were exciting, but it took some time to acclimate. It was a solid six months before I could call anyone there a friend. Each move we made led to another spell of sadness and solitude.

I was a stranger. Every time I became the *new guy* again I felt entirely isolated. I was the kid who said "hello"

and smiled at the bus driver each morning because I knew him; he was part of the fabric of my daily experience. After each move, I was confronted with strangers, people who thought it odd when a young man they'd never seen before gave them a friendly grin and a warm greeting.

I was a kid. I could not possibly have understood at the time that I simply loved people. I could not have understood that I was traipsing blithely through socially accepted boundaries and delving into a level of intimacy that was confusing and confounding to those around me. I certainly did not have the self-confidence to simply be myself and let the chips fall where they may.

It would not be until much later that I would realize that I was already discovering and exploring my personal passion; the passion that was shaping me and would ultimately lead me to a successful career.

Thinking about your passion may spark excitement, fear, love, or hesitation. Do not be afraid of your passion. Accept what makes you feel good, and do not let other judgments interfere with it. This is not about anybody but you. More importantly, don't allow *you* to interfere with yourself. Sometimes, we hinder our own growth or progress because we're afraid of change or failure. You're reading this book because you were attracted to the idea of your passion; don't be afraid now to find it and to activate it. Get ready to enhance your life.

It is incredible to think how many people live day-to-day doing jobs they don't enjoy. We find ourselves comfortable in a routine and simply forget about our lost happiness. If you are caught in your routine, or work in a field you once were passionate about and have realized that your passion has dwindled and your desires have changed, then it is time to recognize that and move forward. If you find yourself thinking about the things that you "should have done" or that you "will do someday," then it is time to pause, survey the landscape, and take action. It is time to do.

I was out to dinner with a small group of people the other night, and one of them asked what I did for a living. I told her that I sold real estate and we got into a small conversation about careers. She was a good thirty years my senior and had worked the same job for the past twenty-one years. When I was speaking about my job, she looked at me with a sense of envy, almost as if she recognized she had no passion for her job anymore as I spoke so passionately about mine. She shifted in her seat and tossed back another glass of wine. "Your career is just beginning. Mine is ending. I am ready to retire," she laughed to herself. The reality was, she could not retire for another five years; however, she was deeply unhappy, bored, and dissatisfied with her current job. I sensed her discomfort and asked her, "What is your passion?"

She thought for a second, unable even to find a passion to which she might put a name. It was her friend, someone who knew her even better than she knew herself, that shouted, "Gift wrapping!"

Immediately upon hearing the words, her eyes lit up and she began gabbing away about how it made her feel so good, so relaxed and energetic. She spoke for four minutes straight without pausing. She was not concerned whether or not any of us at the table were even listening to her. She was not concerned that it might sound odd that gift wrapping could be a passion. She was *in her passion*. It was a beautiful moment to see her light up and live that joy. She admittedly did not understand why or how gift wrapping made her feel so good, but she knew she loved it. The smallest thing is often the unseen passion.

It was immediately apparent to me, and to everyone at the table, that if this woman chose to quit her job and focus her day-to-day efforts on her passion of gift wrapping, she could find a way to make a career out of it and, more importantly, live happily doing it. Why settle for anything less?

Finding your passion is the first step, but activating it is the gratifying part. The amount of success I have encountered in such a short period is attributed to living in my passion. I believe when you activate your passion, external elements are attracted to you like a magnet. New opportunities, people, and situations that normally would not present themselves do so because your passion is activated.

———◆———

My first day as a real estate agent was no different than my first day at a new school in a new town. Just like going to lunch on the first day of class, *I felt naked and judged.* At the age of twenty-four, I was the youngest agent in the office and felt as though I knew nobody. But as I looked around the bustling room full of strangers, I realized this was not entirely true.

I was young, but I was no longer a child forced into a new neighborhood. I had found my way there by exploring my inner workings, by discovering my passion. I might not have known any of the people in front of me yet, but I knew myself. I had chosen to go there. It was time to get on the bus.

I picked out a face that looked friendly enough, extended a hand, and offered a warm grin. Stepping into my passion, I said, "Hello."

And the journey had begun.

CHAPTER 2

I Have To Do *What?*

When they handed me the big boxes of chocolate bars for the school fundraiser, I had a moment of panic. I'd seen those boxes of chocolate before, when my older brother, John, had been in this grade. I remembered how miserably he had lugged his goods from house to house. I remembered him coming home dejected and depressed, with tired, aching legs and boxes of unsold chocolate bars. He had worked so hard, and had wanted so badly to win the bicycle that was given each year to the student who sold the most bars and raised the most money for the school.

I also remembered the kids who had come to our door with their slightly pathetic pitches. They stood there, just outside the house, half muttering a plea for my mom or dad to buy candy bars from them, always with the same half-ashamed explanation that my parents could help them win the coveted prize just by making a purchase. I did not want to be one of those kids.

I sat in my bedroom, staring at the boxes of chocolate bars, and formulated a strategy. The next day, instead of walking door to door, I took my goods to the local news-room and the small, family-owned market down the street. Instead of pitching people on the idea that they could help me win a prize, I talked to the owners of these establishments about the need for band instruments and team uniforms. Because I am who I am, I enjoyed the opportunity to meet all these people who lived and worked in my neighborhood. I enjoyed having an excuse to talk to them and initiate a relationship.

I asked if they wouldn't mind setting a box of chocolate bars near the counter, to help raise funds for my school. I assured them that I would be back each Thursday evening for the next two weeks to collect any money that had been earned. I put the boxes in place, with a small handwritten sign that simply read, "Buy a candy bar. Help raise money for the Chaparral Elementary School." I did the same thing at the dry cleaners, the local diner, and any other shop that seemed to have a lot of foot traffic. By the end of the first week, almost all of the outlets had sold out of candy bars, and many of them wanted to have their stock replenished.

The real estate industry, like most sales industries, is fiercely competitive and challenging. Throw youth and inexperience into that mix, and I was heading down a tumultuous path where success frequently seemed impossible. Getting into real estate was terrifying. I was attempting to penetrate a very exclusive market, where the average home sold for $2.6 million. When I first started working as an agent, I looked at the 275 homes for sale in Malibu and the 300 licensed agents trying to sell them. I wondered how I could possibly fit into that picture.

Fortunately for me, it took a lengthy ten months to receive my real estate license because the state had a complication processing it. This was discouraging at the time, but looking back, the timing of my license was perfect, as divine timing always is. Had it come any sooner, my results might have been different. The extra time gave me ample opportunity to mentally prepare and set my goals. It was an advantage to have ten months to think about "my success" in real estate without being able to actually sell property. I read an immense amount of literature, and studied the Internet and the market zealously.

My first year in real estate was exhaustingly exciting. It consisted of attending computer and software training courses; finding and developing a relationship with a mentor; attending office meetings; going on caravan; meeting with escrow officers, title reps, and lenders; and, most importantly, studying contracts and inventory.

I became a dedicated reader of the local newspapers, paying special attention to the real estate sections. I explored the Internet for websites and articles that provided pertinent information. If I was going to be a realtor, I needed to know how to talk like one. I focused on all aspects of the industry, reading about everything from remodeling to interest rates. I went to functions and listened to others speak about real estate. I struck up conversations with my friends and family members and asked questions in the office. I listened to real estate motivational CDs and attended local workshops. I studied the contracts, addendums, and disclosures required to purchase, list, or lease a property.

I practiced what I call "information sponging." The faster I sponged information, the more confident and resourceful I became. It would not be long before prospects would start to recognize this. Since I was passionate about real estate, my newfound career, this process was energizing.

Information sponging is a necessary step before talking the talk, much less walking the walk. If you are passionate about what you do, then this process should be fun. Take action and learn, absorb, and seek out information. If you are the most knowledgeable person about a specific topic in a room full of people, then you become the authority by default. Becoming a resource is imperative. If your goal is quick success in your career, immerse yourself in it.

I knew a few people in Malibu, but it was not my hometown. My parents certainly were not locals. I did not want to do what my colleagues in the industry suggested: knock on doors, cold-call, and sit open houses. If those were income-producing tasks, why were the *top agents* not knocking on doors all over town? Why were they not sitting their own listings on open house? I thought there must be a more productive and efficient way to attract clients. Besides, I did not live in a community where door-knocking was customary. It was practically illegal to cold-call, and open houses just seemed like a waste of time. I searched for other ways to attract business. I had a degree in advertising and had loved marketing and advertising since I was young. This was an opportunity for me to activate another passion of mine and to grow my business.

Not only was I in charge of marketing myself as a brand in the real estate business, but I was basically running an entire company—*alone*. As an independent contractor and a salesperson, I was essentially acting as CEO, VP of Marketing, VP of Research and Development, VP of New Business, VP of Technology, Secretary, Scheduler, Producer, Sales Representative, and Accountant. That was a lot to handle—but to be successful I had to recognize that nobody was going to do these jobs for me—at least, not for free.

I was overwhelmed. Yes, my business card had a company logo on it that people recognized, but the company paid me nothing if I was not earning commissions. The manager that hired me expected me to make the office money, not to incur additional costs. I had the same expectation, but I wasn't sure *how* to make money. Nobody was holding my hand or offering me the safety net of a regular paycheck if I didn't make sales. If you ever find yourself in a similar position, where the only way you're going to earn a living is if you make it happen yourself, allow me to offer you one piece of advice: Don't be discouraged, be inspired. You can do it. Set the intention today, right now, that you will think positively about your new career involving your passion. Take action. Regardless of what everyone else tells you, go for it. If I had listened to everyone else, I would be a loser, and I definitely would not be writing this book, much less telling you stories of my success as a realtor.

In fact, do yourself a favor and never define the word *failure*. This word is completely subjective; it can only be defined by you if you choose to define it for yourself. However, if you do not define failure, then you cannot fail. There is no negative reaction to your action. If you do not reach your goals, set different goals; make different decisions. Failure cannot be an option if it does not exist. That is the attitude I had when entering the real estate industry, and the one I have for most situations in life.

Sitting in one of the most challenging courses I ever took at Pepperdine, Mass Communication Law, I became convinced that I was destined to fail the course. I can assure you that, had I not had a moment of clarity halfway through the semester, I would have failed. However, I decided to change my attitude and eliminate the possibility of failing. If I saw the class as an opportunity to learn and to grow, and I walked away with more knowledge than I began with, then how could I fail? We have all been indoctrinated through the academic grading system. We are programmed to believe failing is an option. Reprogram yourself to live in a world where all action leads to success. I am asking you to eliminate your definition of failure and replace it with a perspective that sees the positive possibilities. This is about recognizing opportunity. *Every person, every event, and every action in every day is an opportunity to grow as a person and to grow your business.* It is the truth.

For me, in real estate, everyone lives somewhere; therefore, everyone is a prospect. What other business boasts such opportunity? Take this moment and vow to yourself that you will see every day as an opportunity to grow your business. Say it with conviction—believe yourself. Becoming successful is not based on luck, but rather on perspective, perseverance, and passion. Donald Trump says, "Sheer persistence is the difference between success and failure." What drives that persistence is passion.

I sold my first home to a celebrity buyer, an actress. For the purposes of confidentiality, let's call her Olivia Magnolia. It was a $2.9 million transaction and I'd been working in real estate for three months.

Ms. Magnolia was one of our resident guests at the Malibu Beach Inn Hotel, where I served as guest services manager during my final year at Pepperdine and the year that followed graduation. She and her son were guests of the hotel for over a year! They moved into the hotel because her Malibu home was infested with mold. She refused to move back into the house, and sold it before she bought another place to live. I had no way of knowing that she was going to be a future real estate client of mine.

Every morning while working the front desk, I saw her son off to school. During her stay at the hotel, prior to obtaining my real estate license (or any intention of getting one), I remember a multitude of frustrated realtors visiting the hotel; looking for her, waiting for paperwork, or trying to give her a message. She mentioned to me time and again that she missed having a home. Eventually, the two moved out of the hotel and leased a condo on the ocean, but the space was small and she wanted to buy a house.

By this time, I had earned my real estate license. More importantly, I had a personal relationship with Ms. Magnolia and her son. I had connected with them, because that's what I do. That's why I had been successful at the hotel where they stayed. I like people. I connect. I offered to help her find a home. I didn't say that I would help her "buy a house" or "search for a property." Having listened to her over time, I knew what she was seeking. I told her that I would help her *find a home.*

I showed her properties all around Malibu, and most of the agents knew her upon arriving at each home. They all had a story about having worked with her at some point, each attempting to sell her a house, all unsuccessfully. She could be indecisive and would sometimes miss appointments or vanish for days at a time, but I had plenty of time and energy to dedicate to her. I knew she needed a home. She had her issues, but I was determined to help her. It took a lot of patience, but the reward of finding her the right home was overwhelming. More importantly, over the course of this shared experience she became a dear friend. This experience, although at times frustrating, fueled my passion.

———————◆■◆———————

At the end of the month, I brought my piles of money to the school, counted out into neat bundles. When my teacher filled out the oversized Magic Marker bar graph, the winner was obvious. I had sold more than twice as many chocolate bars as Tim Morris, who took the second-place prize, a hardcover Merriam-Webster's Collegiate Dictionary.

They presented me with my prize and I brought it home. A few minutes of work with my dad's crescent wrench to raise the seat and the handlebars and it was exactly the right size. John really wanted that bike. I just wanted to win the competition. Every time I saw him ride up the street on it, I felt a swell of pride.

I know I've mentioned it before, but it bears repeating. My passion is the *people*. Always has been.

1. Do Your Passion

The foundation for success in any field is loving what you do. Being successful takes hard work and long hours, and if you aren't genuinely intrigued by what's holding you captive, your days will seem long.

2. Ignore Negative People

People will inevitably feel the need to impose their personal beliefs and opinions on the choices you make along your career path. Keep your eye on the prize and look at negative opinions as a challenge. Use them to help you set goals and surpass them.

3. Don't Define Failure

There is nothing to fear if there is no definition of failure. Your only option is success because that is the perspective you have.

4. P.O.P.

Look for the positives, find the opportunities, and persevere.

CHAPTER 3

Ready, Set, Go

I drank and did cocaine for a lot of reasons. I self-medicated against loneliness, against depression, against my own sense that my dreams were fading. Intoxicants created an illusion of brighter colors and sharper contrasts in a world that was losing its sheen.

I entered college ready to study advertising, make a name for myself in the world, and carve a legend across the face of an industry! I was young and energetic. I partied with my classmates and we had good, good times. As long as I was able to keep my grades up, I figured everything was fine.

I would wake each day to a blurry world, and each day I would take something to sharpen it back up. One morning, it occurred to me that I was more interested in finding the next party than attending class. My ambition was becoming a distant thing, something seen through the wrong end of the binoculars. I had somehow wandered off my path.

I didn't know what it was that I was looking for, exactly. I didn't even know where to look for a signpost. All I knew was that I no longer felt like myself. I was not the person I wanted to present to the world.

———————— ◆ ————————

Start with the basics. Whether your passion takes you into real estate or car parts or dog grooming or knife sharpening, your reputation begins on day one.

I remember sitting at my desk in the bullpen on my first day of work, watching the other busy agents. Phones rang. Not mine. People ran pages through a copy machine. I had nothing to copy. I wanted to at least *seem* busy. On that first day, I called my mom four times and begged her to not leave her phone in case I found myself with nothing to do at my desk. I wanted the other agents to think I was busy, productive, and active, even though I was new. I wanted their respect.

In the beginning of your new career there is a lot of hard work to be done. It is not glamorous and it is certainly not always fun. If you do the groundwork, though, if you focus on your passion and your goals, everything you do will be in service to the "big picture" idea for yourself and your company.

Take things one at a time. Forming a personal brand image and a personal mission statement are critical. This is standard business practice, textbook advice, and advice that should not be overlooked.

Think of your mission statement as your identity. Make it specific. Let it brand you, and allow it to make you stand out from others. Your mission statement should encompass all aspects of your life, beliefs, and characteristics. It should portray who you are and who you would like to become. Do this truthfully, and it will guide you in times of difficulties, stress, or conflict, as well as prosperity and success. Your mission statement does not necessarily have to be used in your advertising vehicles, but it will create an underlying tone for your style. Be cognizant of who you are and who you want to attract. Capitalize on those attributes.

Think of the beginning of the movie *Jerry Maguire*. It's the middle of the night and Tom Cruise is sitting in front of his computer in his boxers, his face feverish. His fingers tap the keys wildly. After years as a top sports agent, Jerry finally remembers why he became an agent in the first place. It was about the simple pleasures of the job. The honest, weathered face of Jerry's mentor fills the screen, and he says, "The key to the job is personal relationships." This scene is one we all recognize, one we have all experienced—or *hope* to experience. It is the moment at which we set aside the habits of the day-to-day world and return to our own ideals, the lessons we have learned that we hold most dear. To some degree, it is a leap of faith and, as such, it is frightening. If you cannot trust yourself on this, trust me. If you really allow yourself to see who you are beneath all the well-practiced routines of repression and compliance—if you really seek out the person that you have always wanted to be—you will find someone you like. You can become that person. In fact, becoming that person is the right thing to do. *It is the most basic act of personal integrity you can carry out.* To do this, it helps to write down the beliefs that you hold most true. Remind yourself to honor those beliefs, especially when challenges confront you.

Not unlike Jerry's, my mission statement started as a paragraph and turned into a very personal few pages. I wound up with two very different mission statements. The first, a Personal Mission Statement, expresses my mission as a person on his journey through life. Think of it as a general statement of my ethos. It developed organically out of the process of creating my Professional Mission Statement, which I was consciously *trying* to create. I will share both; as you will see, the two are inextricably connected.

PERSONAL MISSION STATEMENT
Be honest with yourself.
Be confident with yourself.
Be happy with yourself.
Respect all things on Earth.
Work hard for your dreams.

PROFESSIONAL MISSION STATEMENT
Be of service to the client.
Be honest with the client.
Be sensitive to the client's needs.
Respect the client.
Work hard for the client, putting her needs before my own.

You might believe that you can just *think* about your mission statement and store it somewhere in the back of your mind, but this isn't enough. You need to write it down. It doesn't matter if you write it with a purple crayon on the back of a napkin—*just write it!* Writing down your mission statement is a commitment to yourself. It also serves as a reminder whenever you feel the need for clarity or inspiration in your life.

When it comes to business, your mission statement will also help you stay true to your ethics. Each deal you make may challenge your integrity, your ethics, and your ability to make decisions. The sad truth is, people will do almost anything to get what they want, especially when it comes to money. It is unrealistic to think that your colleagues and clients will not challenge your ethics. It took time for me to understand this.

Remember that whatever professional realm you enter is also a realm you help to shape. While you learn from your new endeavors and inform yourself on their workings, you also inform the people around you and affect the landscape by your presence. It is important that your clients and colleagues know that you will not practice unethical business. The way you conduct yourself will consequently attract the same types of clients and colleagues. If you work with integrity and firm ethics, you will attract like-minded clientele and companions on your journey.

Not only is it our duty as human beings to be honest and ethical, but being so will also provide longevity to your career. I learned quickly that I was very naïve; almost entirely blind to greed and manipulative business behavior.

One weekend, when I was just starting out as an agent, I received a phone call from a man inquiring about one of my listings. He and his family wanted to schedule a showing at the property right away. I was excited at the prospect of selling the house, so I dropped everything and agreed to meet with them in an hour. After showing the house, it was clear that the man wanted to buy the property. He told me that he had not yet hired an agent, and he wanted me to represent him in addition to representing my seller (dual agency is legal in California).

I thought it was my lucky day. As if I didn't already know, he made sure to remind me that I would be making more money because I would be representing both sides. Figuring that the extra money in my pocket would put me in *his* pocket, he started to ask questions regarding price and strategy that would have effectively caused me to sell out my seller. In addition, he told me that if he could purchase the home for $2.9 million (it was listed for $3.2 million in an incredible seller's market), he would give me one of his cars. He mentioned Porsche, Mercedes, and BMW, waiting for my eyes to light up. He tried to assure me that nobody would know about the car; he would just drop me the keys on the day of the sale. My eyes lit up, all right, but they lit up because I couldn't believe this man was asking me to take a bribe and, more importantly, break my fiduciary relationship with my seller. After getting over the initial shock of the bribe, I looked at the man, with his family in my peripheral vision, and told him that I could not disclose what my client would sell the property for, nor could I accept bribes or gifts. He persisted, pressing onward with a proposition he was sure I couldn't refuse. I listened. Finally, once he had finished his proposal, I simply looked him in the eye and said, "Sir, I am afraid I cannot represent you in this or any transaction. What you are asking me to do is illegal and unethical, and it's not worth it to me." The man was clearly put off and frustrated, and he quickly left with his family. I locked up the house and felt proud of myself. I had set clear boundaries and stuck to my ethics.

No matter how broke or desperate I was, I knew that I did not need or want a client like that. Since then, I have made a conscious effort to avoid clients that I can sense will become energy-suckers. Believe me, there are tons of them out there. However, if you make a point to work with honest and positive people, you will attract them to you in return.

In fact, once I had worked with a few good clients, they began referring their friends and family members. At this point in my career, I am still constantly amazed by the wonderful clients I have, and the most amazing part is that many of *them* have found *me*. One day, two sweet, beautiful college girls literally knocked on my door and asked to buy my house. I told them it wasn't for sale, but that I was a real estate agent and would be happy to help them find a house in the area. They ended up staying on their university's campus and never buying, but I introduced one of them to my younger brother, Wayne, and she became his girlfriend for nearly a year. (He no longer holds the bike I won for my older brother, John, against me; the girlfriend was way better.) It sounds like an unbelievable coincidence, but the more these serendipitous experiences occur, the more I realize that success is about building good relationships, helping people, and working ethically. The universe responds, and these coincidental blessings will at times come knocking at your door.

Your journey cannot just be about making money and contacts, but something much deeper. Each time you set a positive example in your business, you further define your own ethics and draw more into your life that is good, rich, and truly valuable. When you practice positive business, you will begin to notice an energy shift taking place and, as a result, you will encounter fewer individuals who ask you to challenge your ethics. Follow the advice of Albert Einstein: "Try not to become a man of success. Rather become a man of value." Do this and success will be inevitable.

When I checked into rehab at the end of the spring term, my plan was to stay for thirty days and get sober so I could resume my "normal" life and my quest for an advertising degree. When I walked into the facility, I looked around and saw a group of losers; drunks and addicts who had screwed up their lives as badly as I'd started screwing up mine. I was surrounded by people who were suffering from years of destruction, pain, and despair.

As I did the work, though, something happened that was nothing short of miraculous. Those losers transformed right before my eyes. They went from being drunks and addicts to being *people*. And as they became people, I realized that I liked them. I wanted to talk to them, to greet them, and to know them. I wanted to help them. I was one of them.

I learned a new way to listen, to communicate, and to help. I recognized that my true passion was intimately interacting with people and finding ways to be of service; to listen and to help others. It felt good to fulfill those needs.

As I found my way out of the haze of my own addictions, I once again was able to see what it was that gave me joy. I rediscovered my passion.

There I was, dealing with my own problems, trying desperately to break my dangerous and destructive habits. I was surrounded by people who were in crisis, people who were battling their own demons. Still, everything became clear as I turned my focus outward. I began to remember who I was.

I was a kid in a new town. I was starting over again in a strange place. This was nothing new to me. I had done this before. And there they were, all around me. The thing that I always needed, always craved before I took my first drink, and still craved, no matter how much liquor I downed. *People.*

The thing about finding one's passion; the thing that ensures your ability to find joy in even the most mundane aspects of a career based in your passion; the thing about being absolutely true to yourself and to your own inner voice is this—and do not take it lightly, coming from a recovering addict: It is simply intoxicating.

CHAPTER 4

Plan Effectively

When I was in Thailand, I climbed a giant penis-shaped rock. I tell this story partly because it will feed into a point I wish to make, but far more, I tell it because I like saying, "When I was in Thailand, I climbed a giant penis-shaped rock."

This was back when I was still drinking. For those of you who have never been alcoholics, it bears mentioning that sometimes, when one is drunk all the time, things happen that would not be likely to happen otherwise. For instance, one might wake up one day, talk briefly to a concierge who speaks only broken English, determine that one is in Thailand, and then, a bit later in the day, see a huge phallus rising from the sea and think, "I'll bet I could climb that if..." or, "Man, I'd love to have a photo of me standing on top of that thing!" Those who are still drinking might look at such times and think that this is a good thing, because they emerged with a great story. That, however, is a rationalization.

I will come back to this story in a moment. I promise. But for the time being, just know this: I was young. I was drunk beyond reason, and I climbed the great, rough Thai penis rock. I stood atop the boulder surrounded by the ocean and did a small dance. That was really as far as I had thought things through.

———————— •◦• ————————

A business plan is about setting goals and looking ahead at the stepping-stones that will take you toward those goals. My father was Vice Chairman of a Fortune 500 company, where he worked for thirty-two years. He is a master of goal setting, business planning, personal development, and the delicate balancing act of earning a living while still having a life. As children, he and my mother taught me and my brothers that we were capable of doing or becoming anything. He reinforced, "There is no limit to your ability. You can dream big and set high goals." He truly believed in himself and in those around him. Being raised by a man who was goal-oriented and followed a business plan allowed me to structure my initial entry into real estate from a pragmatic approach, without restricting my potential for success. If you were not raised with similar beliefs in your household, take a moment to imagine what it would be like if your father or mother had imposed a similar vision. Be honest with yourself about what restrictions were placed on you and your dreams as you grew up. Let go of those restrictions now. They are not serving you.

In my first week on the job, my business manager gave me a blank business plan to fill out. I worked on it carefully, thinking about my goals. Every time I wrote down my

(From left) Madison, Wayne, Wendy, Phil, and John Hildebrand

Madison and Wendy Hildebrand

dreams, goals, or plans, I got excited. I was thrilled by the end of the exercise and was prepared to get started.

Per my manager's request, I went to his office to share my business plan with him. As I read my plan aloud, he went from a forward-leaning, elbows-on-the-desk, attentive listener to a more reserved position, feigning relaxation, as if he were listening to a long story. He sat back in his chair, his hands clasped behind his head and his mouth open slightly. When I finished and looked up at him, he paused, and then said, "Madison, this is very thorough, but don't you think you should set more realistic goals for yourself? I don't think it's a good idea to set such high goals."

"What? More realistic goals? There isn't anything unrealistic about my goals. Besides, these are *my* goals and *my* business plan. There are no restrictions to those." I was a bit offended, and a little angry. He did not understand that *failure* is not in my vocabulary, just as I did not understand that unlimited success was not in his experience. My business plan was immune to anyone else's personal experiences, limitations, or expectations.

He heard the passion in my voice and quickly shifted to a more supportive role. Still, he remained unconvinced. He was fairly certain that I was setting myself up for failure.

I left his office feeling even more motivated to reach my goals. Now I was not only pursuing my own dreams, following my own passion, but I had the added incentive of wanting to prove to this older, wiser person just what could be achieved if one took a positive approach. It wasn't about proving him wrong. I didn't care about that.

It was about wanting him to lean forward again, to regain his own excitement, his own enthusiasm. I wanted him to be filled with the joy, the passion, and the energy of potential again.

I also wanted to be the Top Producing New Agent in Malibu and break all records at my office. I wished to earn $500,000 in commission by the end of my first year. The truth is, I made $250,000 in commission my first year, not $500,000. Now, a person who focuses on failure—a person who believes in failure—might find one here. This is the power of negative thinking: the ability to look at a two-hundred-fifty-thousand-dollar first year as a failure. To me, though, this was a huge success. I now knew what it took to earn $500,000 and was ecstatic that I was getting results for my actions.

Because I had found work that I was passionate about, I found it easy to create a business plan that went beyond the immediate moment, beyond the first goal. I had found something to which I was prepared to dedicate my time, my life, and my spirit. Having moved through the first year, I remained poised for action, positioned to advance. I was on my way.

Your business plan should be free of others' limitations, expectations, or experiences, and it should be absolutely free of any definition of failure. You are entitled to set goals and strategies based on knowing yourself. This is a time to think big and to think how you will achieve big. Remember, failure is not an option because you do not even have a definition for the word. You are about making progress, making decisions, and making necessary adjustments.

There's a common joke in most Jackie Chan movies that always gets me. He's chasing someone. He runs across rooftops. Finding a gap too wide to leap, he uses a bamboo pole to vault the distance or a discarded board to bridge the gap. At some point during the chase, he misses. He takes a really bad fall. Back down at ground level, he gets hit by a car, or trips and does a spectacular falling roll. As he gets up to continue the chase, someone shouts, "Are you okay?" Chan, continuing the action, shouts back, "NO!" But he does not stop running, does not slow down. His focus is on the chase. Pain, injury, collisions, full-on body blows; these things are just momentary interruptions of his steadfast pursuit of the goal.

In Jackie Chan's case, the goal is to capture the bad guy, retrieve the kidnapped girlfriend, or execute whatever plot device has been set up for the sake of the storyline. But the underlying message is an important one. Fix your eyes on a goal and keep adapting to circumstances. Adjust your course as necessary. Take the hits that come. Keep moving toward your goal.

In almost every success seminar you attend or motivational book you read, the topic of goal setting is addressed. This is not a coincidence. Setting goals is the foundation for a successful business plan. The problem is that, like writing down a mission statement, people assume they can just *think* about their goals and move on to the next chapter. If you do this, chances are you will forget what your *specific* goals are, and months later, when you stop to consider what you've achieved, it will be difficult to measure your success. So, no matter how you have to do it, get your goals down on paper.

Had I not completed my business plan and shared it with my manager, I would have had nothing with which to go back to him a year later. We could not have seen where I met my goals and where I fell short. I would have had nothing in writing on which to base the coming year's plan and calculate how much growth I wanted to achieve. The alcohol and drug rehab I attended also encouraged me to write a life plan, which is synonymous with a business plan. I chose to write my plan and share it with another person. There is power in writing and power in sharing. Setting that intention does something positive in our subconscious and it can only help, not hurt.

Here's the thing about the giant Thai penis rock. Getting to the top was easy. And getting to the top was all that I had thought about. In my drunken stupor, I had imagined that moment atop the upright boulder; a moment that could be captured in a flash through a camera's lens. Looking no further than that, I had pushed toward that moment and had achieved it.

I was drunk atop the rock. Coming back down was a sliding, scraping, falling, clawing ordeal. I fell into the cold sea with hands and knees bleeding, ankles sprained, and muscles sore.

Life is not a fast, easy climb to a single snapshot moment of glory. Life runs longer than that. It is not about swiftly rising and then being frozen in time. Sometimes it is a long, slow trudge, with an occasional pause to look at a spectacular view. Sometimes it is hard work and sometimes it is scraped knees. When it's a wide-open plain, start walking. When it's a tightrope, find your balance. Just keep looking ahead. Take the long view. This is living.

Your business plan should encompass the following three categories:
1. Financial, personal, and business goals
2. Analysis of projected annual business expenses
3. Analysis of your business

Tips for successful goal writing:

1. *Be specific.* Take the time to think about and then write down exactly what you want. If you don't know, how can you ever achieve it?

2. *Set deadlines.* Assign deadlines to each goal. Although you may not reach your goals in exactly the time allotted, setting goals will keep you motivated and on track.

3. *Share your goals.* When you share your goals with others, it puts pressure on you to succeed and reach them. You'll also be surprised how supportive people are, which tends to help you stay motivated.

Set Financial, Personal, and Business Goals

A sample outline is provided to complete step one of your business plan: setting goals and deadlines. In some ways it is specific to the real estate industry, but it can be used as a guide for any career. Just make sure to build your own with personal deadlines and goals. Fill in the blanks.

1. I will earn $_____ during the next twelve months.

2. In order to take care of myself and my family, I will: (example: exercise, take a vacation, plan family activity)

   a. _____

   b. _____

   c. _____

   d. _____

   e. _____

3. I will receive the following achievements for my success:

   a. _____ by (date) _____

   b. _____ by (date) _____

4. I will purchase _____
   by (date) _____.

5. I will prospect a total of _____ hours per week.

6. I will host _____ open houses per week and I will invite _____ homeowners from the immediate area.

7. I will write _____ personal notes to people in my sphere of influence each day.

8. I will work _____ hours per week, with _____ percent of that time being devoted to areas resulting in listings.

Analyze and Anticipate Business Expenses

I'm going to give it to you straight because, when I began my career in real estate, I wish someone had told me what I'm about to tell you: *you will have to spend money to make money*. This may seem obvious, but many people feel shocked and discouraged when they realize that, initially, they are spending much more money than they are making, and may not have the resources to continue working in their chosen field without also working a second job. It's not worth taking the steps toward embarking on a new career and quitting your job, only to realize that you don't have enough capital to get started, let alone support yourself until you start generating a profit. Let this be your opportunity to plan and prepare wisely so you can maximize your success.

To get started in any career, it's best to have enough cash to promote yourself for at least six months, in addition to enough reserves to work without income for the same period. This is ideal, because if you're not financially stressed (or desperate, for that matter), your energy will appear different to clients, colleagues, and anyone else you encounter. You are a better salesperson if you *never need* to make the next deal. You will negotiate better because your agenda will not be distorted by a sense of panic and desperation. Sometimes, this will require that you remind yourself of your larger priorities in order to let go of something that seems critical in the heat of the moment.

Early in my first year as a newly licensed real estate agent, I had a client who desperately needed to complete a deal. His family was to follow him out to the West Coast in a few months, and the last thing he wanted was to move from his tiny rental to a larger rental with his whole clan while continuing to look for a new home. After weeks of searching, he had finally found the house that he wanted to move his family into upon their arrival. The only problem was that the asking price exceeded both his budget and, quite frankly, the market value of the home.

Worse, I very much needed to close the deal. It had been some time since I received my last commission check and I was beginning to get nervous about my own financial situation. Perhaps sensing our weakness, the seller's agent began to dig in his heels, refusing to come any closer to our offer.

I came very close to recommending to my client that he raise his offer to meet the seller's demands, but this would have been counter to my mission statement. This would *not* have been in service to the client's needs. Moreover, I recognized that in fact it was my own desire to close the deal that pushed me toward this decision.

I reminded myself that my mission statements, both personal and professional, forbade me to take such an action. I assured myself that sticking to my ethical standards would pay off more in the long run than any single deal could pay off on the spot. No matter how much I needed a good payday, I was not willing to sell out in order to cash in.

Once I'd put my decision in those terms, I was very calm. I no longer *needed* to close the deal. There would be other deals, other days, and other houses to buy and sell.

I told the seller that my client could not agree to the price he was asking. I apologized for wasting his time and walked away. By the time I returned to my office, there was a message waiting for me. The seller had made a counter offer and a proper negotiation had begun.

It's incredibly important to be able to walk away from a client or a deal that is a waste of your time and energy. As you start a new business, this can be very difficult. Every deal, every new client or customer should feel more like an opportunity than an urgent mission. In order to maximize your own comfort level, and therefore both your ability to behave professionally and your chances of success, carefully gauge what your potential expenses will be in launching your business.

To make certain this advice isn't too real estate-specific, let's consider a different example. Let's say you've realized that your passion is performing cosmetic surgery on turtles and other amphibians. For years you've been working at a vet's office, giving wormer medication to poodles and cocker spaniels, but now you have decided to shift your focus to the frogs and tortoises you've always loved. Here we go.

First, identify the *free* resources available to you. There is no need to spend money when somebody else will do it for you. If the office in which you've been working has room for a specialist, voila! You have a space that's already outfitted with a small operating theater and a great many of the supplies you will need.

You should be ordering the following items: business cards, which may or may not display the logo of your veterinary office, depending on whether that logo is recognizable to the community at large; a website or a link to your own page on your company's website; and a white coat with a little black name tag that identifies you and your area of specialty. Unfortunately, there are many expenses you'll have to pay for out of pocket.

TRAINING CLASSES

Almost any new endeavor will require a certain amount of specialized training. It is likely that you will have to pay a portion or all of the costs for the classes involved

BUSINESS CARDS

If your office manager doesn't provide these for you, you can usually order a box for under a hundred dollars. Make sure you get high-quality business cards on a fairly heavy paper stock. Always make the best possible first impression.

PERSONALIZED SIGN OR SHINGLE

You want to make sure that your name appears somewhere on the outside of the building, and that it is clear that this veterinarian's office has a specialist in shell repair and frog-face reconstruction. You can also include your website address on the shingle, so that passersby know where to get more information about you in case Thomas, their pet platypus, has a horrible, disfiguring bookend accident.

WEBSITE

Regardless of how savvy you are with computers, you need to have a website. Either set up a personalized page using your company's web space, or find a web designer to create your own. This involves a lot of work and can get costly if you're not careful. A good place to find an inexpensive, quality web designer is at a nearby college. Place an ad on the Internet or in the newspaper, or ask the contacts in your network for a referral. An initial design should cost about five hundred dollars, and a monthly maintenance fee should be about fifty dollars. You can always upgrade to something classier and more expensive later if you feel the need.

LIABILITY INSURANCE

In all industries, a customer can accuse a business representative of wrongdoing and claim that the error or mistake cost him money or harmed him in some way. You can limit your personal liability by drawing up a contract with your clients and purchasing liability insurance. This can be very expensive, but liability insurance will become invaluable if a suit is brought against you.

TRANSPORTATION

If you have to make house calls—but let's face it, newt breeders are notoriously reluctant to leave their homes—you should estimate the cost of gas that will be used to get to and from such appointments.

MAILED ADVERTISING

Depending on how many people are in your sphere of influence and how frequently you plan on mailing pieces, your costs will vary. I mailed fifty pieces each month for the first year. By the end of the year, my sphere of influence reached about 150 addresses. In addition, I did not mail $0.49 envelopes; I sent large envelopes and packages that cost about $2.50 each. Not only was the cost to ship $2.50 per piece, the specialized envelope or package cost an additional $2.50. Plus, the high-gloss paper and any item I put inside (see Chapter 12) cost me about $2.00. Keep in mind, I'm in real estate. More people need homes than face-lifts for their salamanders. Your mailing list may not be as extensive and you may not need to spend as much per item as I did, but plan to do regular mailings. When someone needs liposuction for a big-boned tree frog, you want to be the first name he or she remembers. This is also why you'll want to plan a budget for…

ADVERTISING

Find your people. Should you be advertising with posters in pet stores? Should you place an ad in the local newspaper? Should you be distributing flyers at the pet fair? Calculate how much you can afford and then find the most likely targets at which to aim your pitch. It is a good idea to share your advertising plan with your manager and mentor (see Chapter 5).

Remember, you are essentially working for yourself, which means your advertising expenses are your responsibility. It is my opinion that you can spare no costs when preparing to market yourself and your image. Everything from your business cards to your car must exude professionalism. Whatever business you go into, you will incur expenses as you get started. Don't let this deter you. Just make sure you plan ahead and leave room for the unexpected.

Analyze Your Business

Structure your day-to-day business operations. What will Monday mornings look like? How much time will you dedicate to learning the market? Sit down and make an outline of a typical week and month in your chosen business. Maximizing your efficiency is the key to working hard without overworking yourself. You can do this by planning carefully. For example, I designate Mondays for setting up appointments, lunches, dinners, and networking. I like to write a few thoughtful cards every Monday morning. I spend the latter half of the day reviewing inventory and market activity from the weekend. On Tuesdays, you may have office meetings with your colleagues, or leave the office to visit potential clients. Dedicate Tuesdays to learning the inventory and updating your website. Wednesdays might be the day you dedicate to marketing and advertising. Send out your next promotion or plan your next PR move. You get the idea. Write down what an ideal week would look like and match it to your goals. By setting your intentions, you will manifest them into realities.

CHAPTER 5

Choose the Right Company

I straightened my tie. I used the side-view mirror to make sure there was no food stuck in my teeth. I ran through my Interview 101 skills: eye contact, no fidgeting, listen to the questions, offer only the answer to the question at hand, don't talk too much, etc.

I had called the office two days earlier. I spoke to the hiring manager and explained that I was a newly licensed realtor interested in working for the brokerage. I told him that I was certain I could be an enormous asset to his company. Michael Quantos, the hiring manager, agreed to schedule a meeting with me. He was the first appointment of many I'd scheduled with hiring managers.

I walked into Michael's office feeling just a little bit shaky. I was entering a new world and I wanted to make a good impression. I had a great many questions. I had high hopes and lofty ambitions. I also had a secret: I had no interest at all in working for Michael or his company.

Choosing the right company to work for and the right people to work with is a crucial decision. Even though as a real estate agent I am an independent contractor, I still work for a company, a logo, and a brand. Whether you're entering real estate or a different industry altogether, you should consider the following: *a secret to success is working with the dominant company in your area.*

Schedule an interview with each manager at the top several companies in town. Regardless of your contacts or your certainty about your choice of company, you need to interview each manager. Interviewing the manager is important because it will be your first experience negotiating with someone inside your industry.

You are interviewing the manager and the company as much as he or she is interviewing you.

I asked questions about the training program offered by the company, the assistance they might provide to offset advertising costs, commission splits, and so on. Before arriving at an interview, be prepared with a list of questions to ask. Naturally, the questions should be adjusted to fit your area of endeavor. If you are interviewing for a job in forestry and land management, it will make no sense to ask about the availability of an advisor on the escrow process. You should arrive at each interview with a clear sense of what it is you need to know, and expect answers, before you move into contract negotiations.

———————

Michael liked my enthusiasm and admired my tiepin. I made small talk about the photo of his children for a few moments before we began the formal interview. From the moment we shook hands, I knew everything was going to be fine. This was my strong suit, the part where I meet and talk with new people.

Over the course of the next twenty minutes, we found our way into the relaxed pace of a conversational dialogue. He asked questions to find out if I would be the right fit for his company. He asked about the range and nature of my sphere of influence. He wanted to know if I was prepared to spend money on advertising, and who I knew that was buying or selling real estate. He asked about my career goals. I had questions of my own, and didn't hesitate to ask them as we went along.

By the end of the interview, Michael wanted to hire me. I told him that I had a few more upcoming interviews, and that I'd get back to him as I saw what my options were and figured out my intentions. An amazing thing had happened. I had arrived at the meeting looking to practice my interview skills, but because I was open to the experience and allowed myself to connect with the interviewer as a person, I left the office far better prepared for all my interviews to come than I had imagined.

I wound up revising my list of questions, having gleaned a wealth of information about what I should consider as I continued my job search.

Once I opened up to meeting and talking with Michael as a person, and stopped thinking of him as a training exercise or a sounding board, he offered me more than I had anticipated, more than he could know. I followed my passion and—just as it always has, just as it always will—it put me on the right path toward success.

I found myself taking an active role in the conversation, rather than a passive role as the object of someone else's consideration.

———————•◦•———————

To give you a sense of what to expect when you begin interviewing *with* potential employers rather than simply letting them interview *you*, here are the types of questions I asked when I was moving into the world of real estate:

1. **Does your company have a training program? How much does it cost? Will you pay for it? How long is the program?**

   Ideal answer: Yes, BIG Realty Co. offers a two-week comprehensive training program off-site. It will cost you $250, and you must attend from 9 a.m. to 5 p.m. for ten business days. It covers everything from escrow, marketing, contracts, insurance, branding, law, and negotiation. You can speak to Jane Doe, who just completed the program, and ask what she thought of it.

2. **Does BIG Realty Co. assist with any advertising costs? At what bracket of sales does it start participating? Is there a marketing coordinator to help with newspaper ads and Internet placement?**

   Ideal answer: BIG Realty Co. will assist with your personal advertising when you become a top producing agent for the company. We do, however, offer space for individual listings in the local newspapers free of charge. The office has a marketing director who can assist you, free of charge, with placing newspaper ads, designing flyers, preparing mailers, and gaining Internet exposure. I will also place an article in the local newspaper stating, "BIG Realty Welcomes John Doe to the Office." In addition, I will buy your first box of one thousand business cards.

3. **Does the company provide access to office computers, printers, copiers, and fax machines free of charge? Phone lines? Desk space?**

Ideal answer: The office pays for all of these items.

[If BIG Realty Co. does not offer to pay for these items, ask if they will be providing a significantly higher commission split than is standard in your industry.]

4. **What would be my commission split?**

Ideal answer: Your initial commission will be split 50/50.

[Initially, this is the most common commission split at nationally recognized companies. The smaller brokerages may offer a higher initial split, but be wary of what they cannot offer that a national brand can.]

5. **How quickly can I advance to the next tier of the pay scale?**

Ideal answer: That's entirely up to you. The more you sell, the faster you move up the scale.

6. **What if I buy or sell my own property?**

Ideal answer: The company offers a special program if you are buying or selling your own property. Here are the forms. As far as family members' properties, we don't offer a program. Perhaps we can arrange an agreement. Do you have family members in the area? I can offer an 80/20 split to you if your immediate family members buy or sell real estate.

7. **Do I have to pay a training director for my first sale(s)? What if I have a mentor who will train me at no cost?**

Ideal answer: Yes, our new agents are required to work with a training director. You will have to pay him or her, anywhere from a maximum of five thousand dollars to half of your first two deals. Obviously, you should try to negotiate the best possible deal with your training director. If you find a mentor who meets your manager's approval, perhaps he or she can help you with your first buyers at no charge, and your first listings, which you will then split.

8. What is your availability to me as my manager?

Ideal answer: I am here for you to consult on individual deals, to ensure that you have the required forms executed to complete each transaction, and to help you work through difficult escrows and negotiations. I will help you create a business plan and stick to it. I will also try to protect you from getting sued.

9. How many new agents do you hire each year? How many of those agents still work for you at the end of the year? To what do you attribute the success of these individuals?

[This answer will vary depending on the size of the company. You want to be aware of any significant difference—maybe it is a managerial or office-specific problem if the manager hired fifteen new agents but only two are still working successfully. Is the training director the problem? Is the office too disorganized? Or is it simply the individuals being hired? How can you be different?]

10. How does this office compare to the other offices in town in relation to its size? What is the company's overall market share in the area?

Ideal answer: We have been the top producing office for the past three years and are always in search of great new agents to keep our office thriving. This company consistently holds sixty percent of the market share in BIG County. You are working for the best.

[When you are new to your field, working for the best known, dominant company will give you every necessary advantage. The community knows and recognizes the company if it is the biggest, and working for them will help you feel more confident. You can focus on selling the company instead of yourself until you become more successful.]

11. **What will it take to become the top producing new agent at this office? If I become the top producing new agent in one year, will you agree to credit me for fifty percent of my first-year advertising expenses and raise my commission split to the next tier at the end of the year?**

Ideal answer: Based on the history of my management, this will require that you sell $13 million in your first year. If you can sell more in your first year, yes, I will agree to your requests.

[You have nothing to lose with this negotiation tactic, as your manager will probably think it is nearly impossible; however, if you succeed, you will benefit. If you don't, then you are not penalized.]

You will not be the only person asking questions. The manager will have her own agenda before she decides if you are the right addition to the office. Like any other company, she will want to know your prior experience.

But more specifically, you should be prepared to answer the following questions:

1. Who do you know?
2. Why do you think you'll be a good real estate agent?
3. What prior work experience do you have?
4. Have you bought or sold your own home before?
5. How familiar are you with contracts?
6. Do you have a budget to market yourself?
7. Do you have any marketing experience?

A friend of mine reminds me constantly that we are known by the company we keep. As you move into a new career, you bring very little history to bear. If your name is associated with a well-established company, or professionals in your field who are highly respected, you gain credibility through a sort of associative osmosis. The success and statistical history of those around you rubs off on you, and you take on the appearance of a seasoned veteran in your industry.

CHAPTER 6

Find a Mentor

Rex is the most brilliant and wonderful dog that has ever lived. A noble, regal, purebred Doberman/Pointer/Labrador-able shelter rescue dog, he has a fine nose and a winning personality.

A few years ago, just as I was moving into the world of real estate, I found myself at a complete loss. I had just received my real estate license and was looking for a company where I could hang it. I had no income and no real prospects on which to base my fantasies of success. I was afraid I had made nothing but bad choices.

I lay on my back on a Moroccan rug that I picked up in Africa some years earlier and rested my head on the warm, furry pillow that is Rex. He curled around to sniff at my face comfortingly for a moment before settling back into his Sphinx pose, and then slowly allowed his head to droop forward until it rested on his forepaws.

For a few moments, I was acutely aware of dust motes drifting in an angled wash of sunlight. I wondered if Rex was noticing them too or whether he was thinking how uncomfortable and heavy my head was resting on his rib cage. Then the phone rang.

John had run into a real estate acquaintance at a vitamin bar. He told the gentleman that I was a newly licensed realtor, and the man said that I was welcome to call him if I needed advice or support. At that moment, I very much needed advice *and* support.

I met with him the following week in person, and he offered to let me join him on one of his showings. The mentorship began.

After a few more visits and conversations, we became very comfortable together and began to trust each other. He started inviting me to his office to listen to phone conversations and negotiations. I began absorbing the environment. As things progressed and I found a position with a reputable realty company, I spoke to my manager about the possibility of having a mentor instead of using the designated training director. He was open to the idea.

Next, I proposed to my prospective mentor the idea of him mentoring me, officially. I told him that, after having been in his office for a few weeks, I respected the way he conducted business and I honored his integrity and style. I aspired to be like him in many ways. In addition, I shared that I had a few strong prospects that would be selling their homes within the next few months, and I would share those listings with him if we acquired them together. A relationship was born. It ended up being mutually beneficial, both financially and educationally. During the time I spent in my mentor's office, I learned more than any book or class could have taught me.

A mentor is, by definition, "a trusted counselor or guide." Finding a mentor is a crucial step to take in the start of a new career. Every new path involves pitfalls and switchbacks. The help of someone who has walked the road before can be invaluable in finding your way.

Your reputation will make or break you, and in the professional world there is very little forgiveness for human error. Look for someone in your industry who has been successful and is knowledgeable—ideally, someone who is at the top of the field—to mentor and assist you with your career. To find the right match, you must first look for someone you respect in your business. Whose personality would you complement for the next few months? Whose personality would complement yours? Whose ads are you attracted to? Whom do you trust?

If you don't have connections with the seniors in your field, ask your colleagues or training director who would be an appropriate mentor for you. Jobs that involve commissions, as the real estate world does, may anticipate this need and include preset arrangements for commission sharing in the case of a mentored deal.

If you have someone in mind that you would like to be your mentor, perhaps the best thing to do is ask your contacts about her. If you have a mutual contact, your prospective mentor may be more open to mentoring you.

Asking someone to be your mentor is a serious decision on both your part and that of your mentor. It is critical that your mentor can commit to making time for you. Do not choose someone who is flattered only by the idea of mentoring a novice, but is really too busy to act as a support system for you. Your mentor is making a year-long commitment to help guide and build your career. It is likely that, for the first few months, you will spend two or more hours per day with your mentor.

As your career progresses, you will spend less time with your mentor, but will still need to call upon her for specific questions. In addition to office time, consider taking your mentor to dinner once a month so that you can have her undivided attention. This will give you the opportunity to ask questions, share ideas, and discuss situations and conflicts in your business. It is an opportunity to get answers.

Regarding the role of a mentor, there are no guidelines for the mentor to follow as far as what kind and how much guidance to offer you. It is up to you to extract as much information from her as possible without being a nuisance. I remember spending hours in my mentor's office, listening and watching his every move. I listened to how he delegated, how he scheduled appointments, how he negotiated, and how he spoke to business managers, clients, attorneys, escrow officers, appraisers, and other agents.

I suggest that you ask your mentor's permission to observe her throughout the day. Of course, make sure that you offer to step out if she has a private call or personal issue.

When watching your mentor do business, do not speak, interject, or offer your opinion. You must simply act as a silent observer. If you have questions for your mentor, wait to ask them until she's concluded business for the day.

When you begin scheduling meetings with prospective clients, ask your mentor if she is available to join you. Before the meeting, you and your mentor should strategize a likely scenario. Who is going to say what? When will you support each other and when might you disagree?

Your mentor can be very useful in terms of helping you establish outside contacts for your business. You may need to work with vendors or agencies that are new to you. There may be whole realms of exterior support in which you have no connections of your own. A good mentor can smooth the road for you as you chart new territory.

In my field this is especially true. There are many vendors involved in a real estate transaction. There are property inspectors, escrow companies, title companies, attorneys, handymen, etc. Most businesses involve outside professionals to get the job done. They are necessary for your success; the better the relationship you have with them, the better service you will likely receive, which will ultimately benefit your client. Take the time to develop strong relationships with the people who will help you get your job done—don't overlook the secretaries. Another benefit of having a mentor is that you can use her name and say, "My mentor, *Jane Doe*, does business with you and says great things about you as a home inspector. She suggested that I call you and introduce myself. It is my goal to be calling you again in the near future when I sell my first home, so you can inspect it on behalf of my client." Feel free to ask questions about their business, too.

A mentor provides you with information, support, and credibility, and is an indispensable component of success. It is important to know that the mentor you choose is someone who will truly support you. In addition to advising and overseeing you and your work, a mentor should wish to see you succeed and should encourage you along the way.

In addition to having a mentor, working for a premier company and having a great training director and manager are invaluable. Taking advantage of your company's resources and asking for help or guidance from your colleagues, manager, and training director are great ways to learn multiple perspectives. Sometimes, your mentor may be unavailable when you have a time-sensitive question that needs an answer, so having another person or persons whom you trust is crucial.

———————————

On my very first deal, I found myself negotiating against my own mentor. Ms. Magnolia—my celebrity client, my friend, the woman who had missed appointments and pulled vanishing acts on me—had at last found a home. We were putting together a $2.9 million purchase offer. The listing agent was my very mentor. Suddenly, it was a conflict of interest to have my mentor guide me through my first deal. Fortunately, I had a great relationship with my manager. He stepped in and guided me through the negotiation. Mind you, my mentor was the top agent in all of Malibu for more than six consecutive years. I was negotiating against a master and had never done it before. It was up to me to do the best job for my client, and I was lacking the expertise of my mentor. It turned out to be a successful and ethical endeavor for everyone, and my client bought the home for a fair price.

I found myself thinking about all of this just a few days ago. The Santa Ana winds blew into town during a hot, dry spell and fires broke out in Malibu. My home was fine, but there were certainly some anxious times, wondering if I would be forced to evacuate, prioritizing valuables in my mind for a quick escape.

As nerve-wracking as all of this was for me, it was far worse for Rex. He paced through the nights and grumbled, his fine nose picking up the scents of smoke and fear. He howled with the siren every time a fire truck raged past on its way to the nearby blaze.

At last, he lay down on the rug in a polluted slant of late afternoon sunlight and stared at me. It took me a long time to figure out what he wanted, what it was that his sad eyes were pleading for. Once I figured it out, though, I was very pleased to fulfill the need. I went to him and lay down, resting my head on his ribs comfortingly. He snuffled my ear for just a moment and then rested his head on his paws.

For the first time in days, with the weight of my head against him, he was able to nap.

CHAPTER 7

Recognize "New" As an Advantage

A couple flew in from New York to look at properties because they were interested in purchasing a second home. They were staying at the hotel in Malibu where I used to work and the concierge gave them my name. This was one of my first referrals, and I was nervous and excited to have prospective clients. On the day I was to show them properties, I picked them up and within twenty minutes they asked me the dreaded question: "So, how long have you been doing this?"

I thought this was going to be the end of a very short day. They would find out that I was a newbie. They would patronize me for a while and then find an agent who really knew what he was doing. I was going to lose the clients and be humiliated. I said, "Honestly, not very long, but I love it!" The couple looked at each other and smirked. It was obvious to them that I was not old enough to have been in real estate for more than a few years. The reality was that I had been working as an agent for only a few short weeks.

I shifted the focus back to the benefits of living in Malibu. I gave them inside information about the hotel and certain hiking trails, casually making them aware of my intimate knowledge of the area and building their confidence in me. The more we talked, the more comfortable I began to feel; and the more comfortable I became, the more they trusted me. That day was a success, not because they bought a home from me, but because I overcame my fear and created a bond with the couple.

The following year, they called me and said they were coming to Malibu again and wanted to lease a home for the summer. Sure enough, we met at the hotel and found a home for them to spend the summer months.

———————•◄►•———————

You have your mission statement, you've written a business plan, you have a mentor (or are at least in the process of finding one), and you're working for the top company in your area. If you feel like you've overcome the greatest obstacles, you're getting there, but now comes the work.

When you begin working as the "new guy" in a competitive field, you may feel like you're at a great disadvantage to people with more experience. The important thing to realize is that although you may be new, chances are, you are not new to dealing with people, and you are not new to being a functioning person in the world.

Relate to your clients or customers and make them feel comfortable. This is the basic rule of customer service and it applies to any career in sales or service. Another advantage of being new to your business is that you will have recently completed the requisite training courses, which means you're the authority when it comes to new laws, addendums, and technology.

The greatest advantage you have is your desire to succeed, and that you've found a career you can be passionate about. Abraham Lincoln said, "Always bear in mind that your own resolution to succeed is more important than any one thing." Passion is a key ingredient to success. You will have to work hard to establish yourself and gain clients' trust, but if you truly want to succeed, are confident, and work hard, you will thrive.

It is inevitable that people will ask how long you've been working in your chosen field. When asked this question, try to answer honestly and with confidence. Use it as an opportunity to discuss your background before you began your new profession and draw parallels, showing how your previous experience informs and applies to your current work. Take the opportunity to tell them how wonderful your new employer is and to explain that although you've only been in the business "a short while," as your clients they are in the best hands—they have your personal support, as well as that of your mentor and manager, or whomever else you have as part of your support team to oversee and help with every step of the process.

If you have really inquisitive clients, they may ask questions about your past deals or projects. When I hadn't sold any properties on my own yet, I would answer these questions with information about deals I'd been involved with, saying, "I have been through two deals with my mentor, one of them was a $3 million property." I didn't claim to have represented either the buyer or seller, but rather let the clients know that I had listened to and followed my mentor through two of his deals. If someone is uncomfortable working with you because of your perceived inexperience, offer to introduce him to your mentor, and have your mentor take him through the deal. It is still a win-win situation for you; if your mentor elects to work with the client, you will be entitled to a commission or a finder's fee, depending on the arrangement you've worked out previously.

Early in my career, a client called me and said she had a referral; a gentleman who wished to sell his home. The home was a bit messy, a vacant fixer-upper on the top of an incredible piece of land overlooking the ocean. I met the owner at his property for a listing appointment, along with the client who had referred me. He was a retired elderly gentleman and he grilled me with questions for almost half an hour. I was prepared and answered to the best of my ability. He agreed with most of my answers, except my commission. He felt that I should be paid four percent. I argued for six percent. My famous line was born that day: "I am worth more than that!" I used every line in the book to keep my full commission. It was finally agreed that he would pay six percent if I brought him an acceptable offer within sixty days. We chatted more about the price of his home and came to an agreement. Finally, he said, "You know, you are young, but I think you have what it takes to sell this house. I was young once, too. I have a son just a little older than you, and I would appreciate if someone gave him this opportunity. I think you can sell my house." At that moment, it became evident that it didn't matter how young or inexperienced I was; if I knew what I was talking about and showed a passion for what I was doing, people would reach out and help me. It was incredible to go from feeling like my newness was an obstacle to recognizing it as an advantage.

CHAPTER 8

Niche Hunt

I was young and a recent graduate from Pepperdine University. I was (and remain) a sober alcoholic. I went to alcohol and drug rehab in the area three years prior to earning my real estate license. In this position, it would have been easy to see my prospects through a lens of hopelessness. It seemed as though everybody I knew was either too young to be seriously thinking about buying property or was a recovering addict.

I tried to look not at the hopelessness of my prospects, but at the vast number of contacts they represented. I started reaching out to these groups, making myself known and accessible to any student or fellow alcoholic that needed assistance with living. Both groups kept me chasing my tail. The students from Pepperdine frequently changed their minds about leasing off-campus, or landlords would simply not allow students to lease their homes. In addition to unpredictable students, needless to say, the alcoholics and addicts had their own share of problems. They were often late to appointments, had bad credit scores, were in a state of constant emotional drama, and their frequent requests for short-term leases made it challenging to convince landlords that they were going to get paid in full and on time.

———————— ◄► ————————

No matter what business you go into, there is going to be a niche for you. To determine yours, you should answer the following questions: What do you know the most about? Who are your friends and acquaintances? What contacts and abilities do you bring to the table?

Find the right perspective on your situation and you will be free to seize the opportunities your life presents. Your niche, like the persona of a stand-up comic, is not something you necessarily choose by making a conscious decision. It is something you discover when you are ruthlessly honest with yourself about your attributes. You will find that you have baggage, that you bring history with you. At first, it will seem as though some of your history is good and some bad. Once you set aside your judgmental attitude, though, and the remembered voices of people whose opinions no longer need to control you, you will begin to find ways to turn the history that you bring with you into an advantage.

Try a simple exercise... Make a list of those things that you think will most hinder you as you move into your dream career; the things your mind tells you will ruin your chances of fulfilling your dreams. Then, figure out where somebody with those same characteristics might fit into the career you seek. An asthmatic sherpa? Maybe he leads disabled hikers slowly and carefully up small mountains. It's a niche market. A one-armed baseball player? It's happened before. A professional actor who stutters? James Earl Jones is that guy. His carefully trained breath and speech patterns led to his signature vocal sound, and the sound that developed as he overcame his handicap turned into a huge selling point. He found his niche.

Whatever it is that holds you back does so only because you perceive it as an obstacle. Allow yourself to see it as a blessing and discover where it might take you.

Both the Pepperdine students and my friends from rehab were very patient with me. They also helped my career by introducing me to other clients.

I went to rehab to get sober and to change my life, not to think about growing a career. However, eventually I was able to see the opportunity to be of service to a whole new group of clients. Not only could I help them find places to live, but I also knew how to relate to them and their individual circumstances based on my own similar experiences.

Now, this client pool might well be exclusive to the Malibu area and other well-to-do enclaves. It is said that nobody gets sober until hitting rock bottom, but the truth is, different people perceive vastly differing depths as "rock bottom." In Malibu, a person can hit the absolute nadir of misery and despair and still have a trust fund, a nest egg, and the down payment on a five-thousand-square-foot property with an ocean view. I'm certainly not suggesting that your local twelve-step meeting should be your first stop as you begin to launch a new career. My point is simply that all of your acquaintances, the members of every group with whom you associate, will become a viable asset as you figure out how your passion can touch their lives.

Pepperdine was another exclusive relationship I had which other agents did not. In fact, one of my first big listings came from a close friend from Pepperdine whose boyfriend owned a home in Malibu. When she told me that her boyfriend was looking for an agent to sell his property, I jumped at the opportunity to meet with him. I promised her that, no matter what, I wouldn't let business affect our relationship, and that her boyfriend would receive premier representation. I ended up getting the appointment and brought my mentor with me, with the intent that we would co-list the property. It was no easy feat. The owner was a high-powered attorney—a bit of a bully, actually. He had a houseful of taxidermies; African animals that he had "shot himself." There were heads, elephant feet, lion rugs, and more. I was disturbed, but my mentor fell into a confused, dizzy silence. He has been a vegan for twenty years, and seeing those dead animals literally rendered him speechless. There I was, sitting between the hunter client and my mute mentor, negotiating a purchase price and a commission. This was only my second listing appointment. I was so nervous and wrapped up in the task at hand that I remained completely unaware of my mentor's disgust and angst. I thought he was just giving me the chance to speak and negotiate. Nevertheless, it was a success. We got the listing, and at six percent, no less! As we left the property, my mentor vowed that he would never show the property himself. This became my first hands-on listing from beginning to end. It was a huge boost to my career, not only because it was my second listing in a few short months, but also because it began to define my niche.

The property was a small ranch home, with plans and permits to build a larger home. It took me a while to realize it, but I had stumbled into another niche—investment-minded buyers and sellers.

These investment-minded clients like to crunch numbers, minimize risk, calculate appreciation opportunities, strategize deal making, and survey the market and neighborhood for signs of deterioration or growth. They are people who enjoy remodeling, renting, and flipping real estate. I, too, enjoy crunching numbers, and I am patient with people. I never try to pressure clients into a decision, but rather offer them the facts and information to allow them to draw their own conclusions. Once I discovered this more profitable niche, I began to develop a business plan that consisted of statistics and results, as well as a strong marketing outreach plan. I began studying the MLS (Multiple Listing Service—website database for realtors to post and access property information) for bargain properties. When I found one, I would call upon my pool of investment buyers. Having found this niche, I did the research necessary to serve the clients who had begun to find me. This fit perfectly with my mission statement. I was simply doing the work that would position me to best serve the needs of my clients.

I also started to attract clients who required a lot of patience. I found myself selling the nest eggs of elderly couples or helping them buy or lease properties. I spent a great deal of time helping first-time homebuyers, usually students who were buying houses with the assistance of their parents. They required an immense amount of patience and explanation. With these types of buyers, the fact that I was new to the real estate world actually worked to my advantage. Because I was just beginning to learn real estate jargon myself, I was able to explain certain terms and concepts in a way they understood. Don't ever forget: there is strength in every weakness, and using your perceived disadvantages to your advantage can make all the difference, especially in your first year of a new career.

Most agents would have looked at the group that populated my world and snorted in derision and disdain. College students and partygoers? Who are you going to sell a house to at *that* party? Instead, I looked at the group and said, "Hey! Look at all those people who have nobody to sell them a house! I can help them out."

Have I mentioned that I really love people? Whenever I can remember that—whenever I can see the world through the bright, rosy lens of my passion—the path before me becomes clear.

CHAPTER 9

Listen and Communicate

I had my license. I had ambition. I had drive, sobriety, and the bright, clear weather that makes Southern California the envy of every winter-chilled Midwesterner in a down-filled coat. I also had one other thing, a thing that terrified me: my new prospect, who was a total stranger to me. And she wanted me to pick her up the following morning to search for the perfect house.

A few years earlier, I had been in the opposite position. My brother, John, was joining me as I looked for a new place to live that would allow me to move off the Pepperdine campus. We waited to be picked up by the real estate agent who was to show us houses. We stood by the curb doing the things that brothers do when they have nothing to do but wait. We laughed and joked and talked about the perfect house. Then the real estate agent pulled up.

Her car was nearly ten years old, and did not appear to have been washed since the moment it came off the assembly line. She seemed startled for a moment when she realized there would be two of us riding with her.

She made the adjustment quickly, though. She put on her best winning smile and said, "Let me just move some of this crap to the trunk for you." We waited a bit longer while she moved what looked to be a half-broken desk destined for Goodwill from the back seat to the trunk, creating enough space for John to scrunch in next to the stack of old *Los Angeles Times* Sunday Editions that took up the middle of the back seat. The remainder of the back seat was occupied by a large Hefty trash bag that bulged with something heavy-looking. Maybe it was a whole lot of dry cleaning. Maybe it was the body of a young man. No way to know.

I slid into the passenger's seat up front, kicking water bottles and old PennySaver coupon books aside to make room for my feet.

As the realtor walked around to get into the driver's seat, John leaned forward and said, sotto voce, "So far, I feel this is going *very* well."

She started the car and we sat there for a while as she checked her map, muttering to herself as she did so. At one point, I offered to help her find what she was looking for. Lost in concentration, she shushed me abruptly.

We pulled away from the curb and drove off down the street. We made several turns, up narrow, winding streets and down again, through residential neighborhoods. When we found ourselves at the end of a cul-de-sac and she unfolded the map again, I knew we were hopelessly lost.

She leaned out through her window to ask a dog-walker for directions.

We looked at a few homes that day, none of them quite what I wanted. She knew very little about other properties that might be available in the area.

After several hours, I said, "I'm getting hungry." And then her car ran out of gas.

The key to success is being able to relate to your clients or customers so that you can help them get what they want. Clients need to feel comfortable talking to you, being with you, and listening to you. Half of it has to do with your personality, and the other half has to do with knowledge. Great salespeople shine because they are confident, sociable, and knowledgeable in their field.

No matter who you are, how you dress, or how you speak, there will be a clientele that feels comfortable with you. Don't make the mistake of choosing an area of expertise simply because it is where you think you'll make the most money. The most important thing is that you *understand* the people with whom you'll be working.

Once you have found your niche (and you may find more than one), make the necessary alterations in order to fit the profile of a person who is successful serving that group. Remember, you are new and inexperienced, but your persona—the "you" that the world sees—should exude confidence and professionalism. I work in Malibu, a casual community. Still, I dress in a blazer with a buttoned shirt, slacks, and nice shoes, as opposed to the beach shorts and sandals that some other agents wear. Whether I am showing a property to an elderly couple or to a younger, hipper first-time buyer, I always want to dress and act professionally. This makes my clients feel comfortable, and it also makes me feel at ease. If you dress well and present yourself in a way that suggests you are successful, people will perceive you as successful. American social critic Christopher Lasch nailed it when he said, "Nothing succeeds like the appearance of success." As shallow as this may sound, if you imitate your clients and customers, they will feel more comfortable with you. Yes, it is a superficial world, but it is also part of the game. The game involves perception. If you are opposed to changing your wardrobe or are uncomfortable in dress clothes, then perhaps you should explore a different niche or demographic. There's someone out there for you to serve, someone for whom *you* are ideally suited. You just need to find the market base that's right for you.

Perhaps the most important factor in determining how successful you will be is *knowledge*. The more you know about your business, the more valuable you are to your clients. As a real estate agent in Malibu, people expect me to have expert insight into the local area. But since I wasn't a Malibu native, it took me some time and effort to really get to know it. It was a lot of work, but definitely worth it. I did research and talked to as many people as I could to learn the inner workings of the community. What schools are in the area, and what are their reputations? Are there hiking trails or dog parks nearby? Where are the closest grocery stores, shopping centers, exercise clubs, dry cleaners, and post offices located? Are there any hospitals or clinics in the area? Are there any prominent organizations or weekly meeting groups? I found out as much information as possible so that I could provide pertinent information to specific clients, depending on their needs and interests. Knowing the area not only established me as a credible resource, but it also helped me connect with people in the community. In the process of acquiring information, I had the opportunity to establish many valuable contacts, and I learned my way around as thoroughly as if I had lived in Malibu my entire life.

When it comes to personality, being likeable is mostly about being patient, present, and confident. Be sure not to confuse confidence with arrogance. People want to work with someone who knows what he or she is talking about, but is also good at listening to others and helping them meet their needs. In the words of Jim Rohn, an American entrepreneur, "You don't get paid for the hour. You get paid for the value you bring to the hour." This quote could not be truer. In real estate, this means listening to your clients precisely, so you will not waste time showing properties that do not meet their needs. The sooner you find the right property, the happier both of you will be.

If you're having trouble relating to a client because of a personality difference, ask questions. Most people enjoy speaking about themselves and find it comfortable to do so. You do not have to ask anything personal, just get the client talking. Look at her jewelry, clothing, car, or anything that might signify a topic to discuss. If she pulls up in a BMW, ask how she likes her car. *Do not talk about yourself* unless you're specifically asked a question. Nothing is worse than being stuck in a car with a realtor who does nothing but talk about his family, his vacation, his problems, etc.

People tend to relate best to other people who are like themselves. One of the learned talents of salesmanship is to subtly mimic your client's jargon by interjecting phrases she will relate to. If your client is a CPA, say something like, "This home is in a *precise* location to the schools, market, and town. This floor plan *really adds up* to a great design for a family." You will be surprised how effective these casual word choices can be in making your client feel comfortable with you. People will feel like you understand them and will be more inclined to continue working with you, resulting in more sales. It is important that your clients respect and relate to you and know they can rely on you to provide them with the best service possible. These little tricks are not deceptions or manipulations. They are the essence of good service.

Being well organized, ethical, and punctual are some of the foundations of success, but the ability to charm your clients and convince them of your competence is the element that will dictate the level of your success. This is all part of instilling confidence in your clients and dispelling their anxieties by sharing your strengths.

The day before I was to pick up my prospective buyer, I went out and bought a BMW. A nice one. A new one. It was a huge purchase, but I figured that clients were going to see my car, not my home. I had a nice little place where the rent was affordable, but I wanted my car to exude professionalism and make my clients feel comfortable.

When I picked my client up at her home, I wanted to be sure that I was driving the car she *expected* to see her realtor driving.

As she slid into the passenger's seat, I said, "I've got some snacks and bottled water, in case we get tired or hungry. Just let me know if you need anything." She smiled at me and said, in a grandmotherly tone, "Aren't you sweet and thoughtful. I'm fine for now, thank you."

As she fastened her seatbelt for the ride, I thought to myself, "So far, I think this is going very well indeed."

CHAPTER 10

In the Client's Shoes

Sarah had chosen Pepperdine because of a picture in the brochure and because she wanted to be far away from her parents. But now that she was in Malibu and looking for a place to live, fear and doubt had begun to set in. She had never been away from home before, she told me.

As we drove from place to place, she talked about the town she grew up in back in Michigan. She told me about her high school and her friends. She told me about her parents, and how supportive they'd been of her decision to come to Malibu, and of her awareness of the doubts and fears they had been hiding in order to remain supportive.

Sometimes she just rode in silence, staring out at the houses or the sea, taking in the new, alien landscape.

Establishing a client base is of the utmost importance. In order to most effectively recruit prospective clients, you must think from their point of view and be able to anticipate any concerns they may have. Take every opportunity you can to understand the client's perspective and the various considerations he or she will grapple with. When a person is looking for an agent to represent her, or somebody to do business with, there are many factors she must consider. Knowing what others are looking for will help you cater to their desires.

To get ahead of your competition, think as if you were a prospective home buyer or seller. Where would you start if you were in their shoes? What would be your questions and concerns? Below is a summary of the clients' perspective, which will assist you in positioning yourself to receive new business.

The Right Company—The world is shrinking. The Internet makes it possible for consumers to research and do business with faraway companies more easily than ever before. As mentioned earlier, finding the dominant company in your area has its benefits. For one, it can afford (and probably has) a large Internet presence, a widespread advertising campaign, and name recognition—more so than a mom-and-pop business. Alliance with such a company can only benefit you as you move into a new field.

Local Presence—Although clients might want to do business with a large company, they will still desire a local presence. Email and telephone conversations are all well and good, but ultimately you'll find yourself working with people who live and function in your immediate area.

Availability—Clients must be able to easily reach the folks with whom they're doing business. Nothing is more frustrating than needing answers to questions or trying to schedule an appointment and having calls go unreturned—or, worse still, having phone calls not answered at all. Make sure you can be reached by landline or cell phone; or, at the very least, ensure that your phone line is covered when you're unavailable.

Basic Professionalism—Always be professional and well-groomed, punctual, and reliable. Keep yourself informed and knowledgeable about the market, and be ready to provide a detailed marketing plan and results to back up your claims.

Experience—Clients naturally feel more secure working with a professional who has been through the process before and can act as a guide; a seasoned advisor; a sherpa, if you will.

Commission—If your industry is commission-based, be aware of how commissions are perceived. Some clients will always want to pay the lowest possible commission. Some will recognize that a lower commission can often equal less service.

Reputation—Clients will, at the very least, Google you. They will also learn about your reputation through friends and colleagues. Be constantly vigilant. Maintain good working relationships, and foster your reputation as a hard worker and an ethical person in every way possible. Even better, provide a list of references and letters of recommendation so clients can confirm your qualifications.

Chemistry—It's important that provider and customer get along, because they may be working closely together for a long while.

As a newbie, you can't avoid the fact that you're inexperienced and haven't built a reputation for yourself in your chosen field...yet. However, simply knowing where your clients are coming from—what concerns they might have, and what common questions they share—allows you the opportunity to address as many concerns as possible. This alone will give you an advantage over most beginners in your field.

—•◦•—

I listened to Sarah as she talked and took in her anxiety. Finally, I said, "You moved here because you liked a picture that you saw. But you can't live in a snapshot. Forget about views and floor plans for the moment. Let's just look around until you realize, and feel, that you are at home."

She nodded slowly, staring out at the seafood restaurants and stucco houses that line the Pacific Coast Highway. Then, so softly that she might not even have been aware that she was saying it aloud, she worked the word out of her mouth. She said, "Home."

Like her parents, Sarah had her own doubts and fears about coming to Malibu. She hid them as best she could—from me; from herself, even—but there they were nonetheless. She had come to a new place; a place where she knew nobody, where she felt disoriented and alone. I asked her questions and let her talk so she could feel as though at least one person in Malibu was getting to know her. And as we drove through the streets, up and down the hills surrounding Pepperdine University, she began to get her bearings. At one point, she said, "Make a left here," and I did.

We took a road that wound up from the PCH, and when we reached the top she asked me to stop the car. She stepped out and moved away from the road until she could look out at the ocean. I followed her, half wondering if she had somehow known of a place for rent on this hidden patch of land.

We stood together in silence, staring out at the sea. Then, she gasped and pointed as a small school of dolphins moved past in the distance, leaping between the waves and blowing little snorts of spray into the air. I said, "Wow. Nice."

When they were gone, Sarah said, "Yeah. Nice. I think it's all going to be okay."

"Yeah?" I asked.

And she said, "Yeah. I think I can live here."

I looked around at the little patch of barren ground, with the scrub growing up through the rough dirt, and said, "Well...not *here*. But close enough to come here when you want to."

She laughed and headed back to the car. I stood for a moment, staring out at the ocean, loving the distant dolphins that had come to welcome Sarah into her new life away from her family. But she was already moving on, and she called back to me, "Come on, Madison! We've gotta find me a home!" And that is exactly what we did.

CHAPTER 11

Networking

I had a neighbor who used to speed-walk by my house every morning. She had her earphones in and she jammed along to her iPod, her hips snapping back and forth in that odd, steam-engine way that a speed-walker's hips snap back and forth.

Every time I saw her, we exchanged smiles. One day, we finally spoke and I told her that I was in real estate. She asked a few questions about the market, but did not tell me that she was thinking of selling her house. As I listened to her questions, though, it became clear that she was thinking about moving.

I was still very new to the business, but I recognized her as a prospective seller from the questions she asked and the concerns she tried to conceal. I hoped that she might become my client and pondered on how to further our relationship. I thought to myself, "How am I going to connect with her and move from the friendly neighbor relationship to a trusted professional relationship?"

I said nothing about that at the time, though. This was going to take timing, careful thought, and planning.

I thought for a few days and determined that my neighbor was a dedicated speed-walker, for whatever reason. I went online and purchased a pedometer that she could wear on her wrist to keep track of her mileage. When the package arrived in the mail, I kept it in my car so that if I drove past her I would be prepared. Within a few days, I was driving up the hill to my house when I saw her headed in my direction at her usual hip-snapping clip.

I slowed down and stopped, smiled at her, and said, "Hi! I saw something the other day and thought of you. I had to buy it, because you're so dedicated to speed-walking I figured this would be a valuable tool for you." I gave her the small gift through my car window.

She was shocked! She was so elated that she pulled me from my car and gave me a bear hug—regardless of her very sweaty body. Two weeks later, she found my number and called to tell me that she and her husband were planning to sell their home. She told me that her husband had scheduled listing appointments with four other realtors in the area. She got me an appointment with her husband, but said she could not promise anything more than that.

I was ecstatic!

This was the first time I was planning to do a listing appointment solo, without my mentor. All week I prepared; I listened to listing presentation scripts and practiced my presentation aloud in front of the mirror. The day of the appointment came, and I was so nervous that my palms were sweating. I drove the neighborhood three times, studying all the houses. Parked in front of my neighbor's house, I replayed the scripts and advice I had received during the week before deciding that I was ready to go in for the appointment. My nerves were shaky, partly from excitement and partly from uncertainty. Either way, I had already convinced myself that this was going to be a great learning experience.

Networking, or prospecting, is an essential component to your success. For me, this is one of the most engaging parts of indulging and fulfilling my passion. The more opportunities I have to meet people, the happier I am about what I'm doing as a career. Fortunately, as a realtor it is a simple and undeniable mathematical certainty: *more contacts = more exposure = more opportunity.*

Seneca, the Roman philosopher, told us, "Luck is what happens when preparation meets opportunity." Some things haven't changed over the course of a few thousand years. Prepare by working hard, making an extra effort to meet people, and getting involved in your community. The reality is that if you are not meeting new people, or your sphere of influence isn't spreading the word about you, your business isn't growing. If you want to be successful, recognize that you are in the business of knowing people and making as many positive and lasting connections as possible.

Before you begin looking for new contacts, keep in mind that referrals are one of the best ways to build your business. Some of the most important people to network with are former clients and associates from previous jobs. If they had a positive experience working with you, they are likely to refer clients to you. To help you begin building your network, review the following list and write down any and every name you think of when you read each entry. Next, track down the address, phone number, and email address for all. Begin to categorize.

1. Parents
2. Siblings
3. Grandparents
4. Aunts/uncles
5. Cousins
6. Teachers
7. Fitness trainer
8. Hairstylist
9. Friends
10. Former boss
11. Former colleagues
12. Owners of restaurants you frequent
13. Owners of shops you frequent
14. Family friends
15. Friends' colleagues/clients
16. Local hotel managers/concierges
17. Neighbors
18. Investors
19. Other business owners

Once you have a substantial list of contacts and resources, and have let each of them know that you're working in a new field and are available to help them with their needs, the next step is to start expanding your network. This may seem overwhelming at first, but keep in mind there are potential clients everywhere.

In my case, I realized that everybody lives somewhere and needs a house or an apartment to live in; therefore, everybody's a prospect. Whether you're getting your morning coffee at the local shop, picking your child up from school, vacationing in Hawaii, or getting your car washed, an opportunity to grow your business awaits.

Opportunity is everywhere. I deliberately visit the local Starbucks every morning, partially because I'm addicted to caffeine, but mainly because it is the watering hole in Malibu. I've discovered that while waiting in line for my Venti Triple Vanilla Latte, endless opportunities arise to make new acquaintances and renew old ones. Most of the people passing through the morning rush at the coffee shop are residents of the community and therefore perfect prospects. I make it a point to always grab the door and hold it for anyone who is entering or exiting. This is a great conversation starter. The first conversation may be brief, but the seed has been planted. It is likely that you will see him or her time and again. Each time, make a point to wave or touch on a point made in a previous conversation. Over time you will build a strong acquaintance. The more people you know, or who know you, the more likely it is that a transaction will result. Each time you meet someone, your first thought should be, "How can I help this person?"—not, "How can this person help me?" Exercise this formula and people will automatically view you as a resourceful and useful contact.

Once you have developed a relationship, it is important to find a way to *thank, invite,* or *help* the person. People love to be invited to events, they appreciate being thanked, and they respect those who go out of their way to help them. I recommend making it a practice to write one charming note per day. It only takes a few minutes and a single stamp, and you wouldn't believe how much this can help cultivate business relationships. For example, a simple phrase that I've had great success with is, "Think good thoughts."

In addition to making networking part of your daily routine, it's essential to expand your web of contacts by becoming involved with at least two regular activities outside of your specific career. This is a great opportunity for you to get involved with another extension of your current passion or to explore one that is not based on building a career.

For example, you can join an exercise club, find a new hobby, join a nonprofit group, go to city council meetings, volunteer your time at charity events, host a party, attend church or spiritual services, or go for drinks at a local restaurant. Every business is about networking your advocates. Those who support you and believe you are a great asset will refer business to you. All it takes is one solid new contact per week to manifest multiple new opportunities. By obtaining at least one contact per week, your Rolodex will grow, your sphere of influence will expand, and referrals will start coming to you. It's essential that you consistently stay in communication via phone, email, or mail with these new prospects and contacts. They will need constant cultivating in order to keep you as their preferred reference for your industry.

Personally, I joined a local nonprofit organization whose vision I shared. It was a new organization that was soon to have a formidable presence in town. In the process of trying to accomplish our mission, we constantly had to reach out to the community. We hosted events and fundraisers that were frequently featured in the local newspapers, stating the "good" we were doing and showing pictures of our group. The community saw this, and it opened up hundreds of conversations with people I would not normally have interacted with. Each event posed a new opportunity to form relationships with community members. I did not join the group necessarily to sell homes to its members, but rather to be a part of an organization that benefits the community. I shared a passion for its mission, which was greening up the public spaces of Malibu. If, as a result, business was procured, then it was simply a bonus.

Most importantly, by joining this organization I developed relationships with people in the community that I otherwise wouldn't have met. People started to know my name and face; they began to associate me with real estate. As a result, my reputation strengthened and my list of contacts quickly grew.

As you fill your Rolodex, it will become more challenging to follow up with your new contacts and increasingly difficult to remember each one. Keeping a brief and organized contact database is crucial. I use a Samsung Galaxy, powered by Google, to synchronize my contacts and calendar. It is important to input as much information as possible about each new contact. I usually make a note as to how we met, where we met, and what we spoke about, to make it easier to remember later. There is no particular customer relationship management (CRM) system that is necessarily right or wrong. One agent in my office, my mentor, sells more than $250 million in real estate each year and uses an old-fashioned day planner.

Other top agents use www.topproducer.com (this costs money). You may need to try a few different systems to find out which works best for you. The important thing is to stay organized and not disregard any potential bond you have formed with a prospect.

I knocked on the door and my new speed-walking friend answered. Just inside the door, I saw a big bowl that held two sets of keys, a man's wallet, and the wristband pedometer I had purchased online.

We toured the house, and then we sat in the family room to discuss price, contract, and so on. Overall, I felt the appointment went well, although I wasn't completely prepared for the depth of some of the questions I was asked.

The discussion regarding the listing price was particularly difficult because of the clients' emotional ties to the property. They had built their original home from the ground up and lost it in the Malibu fires of 1993. They rebuilt their home and poured their hearts into it. They felt that their home was worth $3 million. Based on market value, I knew that it was worth approximately $2.6 million—and even that might be a stretch! They told me that another agent had valued their home at $2.995 million. I told them I disagreed, and said that I would list their home for no more than $2.75 million. It was very difficult to stand firm in my belief, despite the possibility that I might lose the listing simply because they felt their home was worth more. However, I felt they respected my honesty. After I left the appointment, I wasn't convinced they were going to hire me, but I didn't want to lose the listing, so I called the following evening and told them how excited I was about the possibility of listing their beautiful home. I shared that I had told my mentor about their property and he was hoping to meet them.

We immediately scheduled another appointment. During the second meeting, the couple asked my mentor the same questions they had asked me. Being a top producing agent in Malibu, my mentor was able to answer their questions with professional finesse, and the couple ended up signing on the spot for $2.65 million. We sold the house within sixty days for $2.5 million.

It was a terrific first step as a listing agent. Sometimes, a single step begins when you notice someone else speed-walking a thousand miles.

CHAPTER 12

Get Noticed...Consistently

The phone rang. It was the director of my company's training program. "Hey," he said, "you wanna come talk to the newbies?"

I had been in the real estate business for eight months, and he wanted me to educate the newly licensed agents on how I had achieved so much success in such a short period of time. He was looking for a highly motivating, energetic presentation to inspire them to succeed as well.

The phone rang. Forbes.com wanted an interview.

The phone rang. *E! News*, *The Los Angeles Times*, KNX radio, and Pepperdine University—all wanting interviews, stories, commentaries, or public speaking engagements. I took everything that came my way.

The phone rang again. This time, Bravo Television was on the line. They asked me to appear in a real estate docudrama called *Million Dollar Listing*. I was to do my job, and they would film me doing it. The show was a success, and suddenly I wasn't just a realtor—I was a *celebrity* realtor!

Learning how to market yourself is crucial to your immediate success. It is vital that you demonstrate your dedication to your new career. Within one month, all of your family and friends, as well as the people in your community, must know that you have started a new career. It is your responsibility to convince them that you are serious and excited about your new venture. Leo Burnett, one of the most successful advertising gurus in the country, said, "A good basic selling idea, involvement and relevancy, of course, are as important as ever, but in the advertising din of today, unless you make yourself noticed and believed, you ain't got nothin'."

I attribute most of my success to a thorough, consistent, and organized marketing approach. At the age of twenty-four, working as a new and inexperienced real estate agent in Malibu, competing against more than three hundred other agents, surrounded by multimillion dollar properties in an area saturated with successful people, I needed a marketing approach that would set me apart from the rest. As a result of creating an organized and professional marketing plan, within months of my introduction to the real estate world, my name and brand started appearing all over Malibu. There was a buzz in the community, and people started wondering how and why I was seemingly everywhere. Prospects, friends, and shop owners were all talking to me about real estate—every place I went, real estate became a natural subject.

The following sections will guide you through a phased marketing plan, and will offer sample letters, branding ideas, public relations and press ideas, exposure techniques, and image portrayal tips. You can alter or enhance these to fit your chosen field of endeavor; however, be consistent and professional.

Preparation

1. Ask your manager or office administrator to submit an article to the local newspapers announcing your new position with the company. Provide your credentials so he or she can write an inclusive and informative paragraph. Also, if you are bilingual, be sure this is included in the article. The announcement should be congratulatory and positive. It can also include your headshot, so that people will recognize your face along with your name.

2. Organize your contacts by separating them into three groups: Personals (family and close friends), Acquaintances (shop owners, teachers, colleagues, etc.), and Similars (people who may not know you, but share similar experiences such as graduating from the same college). Make sure that all names are spelled correctly and current mail and email addresses are included. For future use, print at least four sets of labels for all of your contacts. When mailing packages, be sure to include your return address, but *do not* mention your company name or "real estate" anywhere on the packaging. By keeping the packaging anonymous and colorful, there is a better chance that the recipient will open it without any predetermined conclusions.

3. Hire a professional photographer to take a studio photo of you. In addition, have the photographer snap a few photos from around town, capturing the symbolic views that are associated with your area. This may include a pier, clock tower, or main square. Get all images on a CD or flash drive in high and low resolution.

4. Order supplies.
   a. Business cards
   b. Mailing supplies
      i. www.containerstore.com. Search "gift mailers." Pick the color that best represents your company and order enough to mail one to each person in your contact database.
      ii. While you're at the website, order bubble wrap mailers in the same color and quantity as the gift mailers.
      iii. www.clearbags.com. Order 9 x 12 inch colored paper envelopes and 9 x 12 inch colored plastic envelopes.
      iv. www.crane.com. Order personalized half-sheet stationery for your charming notes. Don't forget to order matching colored envelopes.
   c. Mouse pads
      i. www.custommousepads.com. Order mouse pads that include the most symbolic image of your town (the photographer should have already given this to you) and your website's domain name. Order enough to mail one to each person in your contact database, and personally hand

out extras around town. These will be a hit, so order plenty.

d. Hire a web designer to begin building your website. Have the web designer buy your domain name (i.e., www.your-name-here.com). Choose a name that's easy to remember, say, and spell. Your domain name doesn't necessarily need to include your name or the words "real estate." If you keep it broad, you can market the site as a resource for both the community *and* real estate prospects. Considering that most people looking for a home use the Internet as part of their initial search, it is essential to have an online presence. Once you have bought your domain name, start building your website by doing the following:

   i. Write the "About" section for the website and send it to your web designer.

   ii. Send your web designer the professional images of your town provided by the photographer.

   iii. Start collecting and writing information about your community, as well as relevant and positive news articles to incorporate into your website.

   iv. Do thorough research so that you can post a community calendar and restaurant guide on your website.

   v. As you begin to build your website, make it your goal to have it completed within one month.

5. Write an "Announcement Letter." You need three variations; one for each category mentioned in step two. Here's an example of how such a letter might look:

Dear Mr. Jacobs,

I wish to tell you of my new job with BIG Realty Co. as a full-time sales agent. I am selling real estate, I am new, and I am reaching out to my friends and family. This business is largely based on referrals; if you know of someone who is moving into or out of town, please let me know. By referring me, you can be assured that he or she will receive professional, ethical, and diligent service.

Furthermore, if there is something I can do for you and your business, please feel free to request it.

I hope this letter finds you healthy.

Be well,

Madison Hildebrand

a. In addition to your announcement letter, include a copy of the newspaper article that was published by your office announcing your arrival to the company. Paperclip the two items together with one business card (giving out more than one business card is not tasteful—besides, you will be mailing more items in the months to come). Now, roll the items together and stuff them inside the gift mailer.

b. One week later, follow up with an email to everyone on your contact list. The subject line should read "Follow up." The email can be very similar to your announcement letter and should mention that you "hope he/she received your package." Be sure to blind carbon copy (Bcc) each person, as it appears to be personalized, and nobody wants his or her name or email address revealed to the other contacts in your address book.

c. Wait three weeks to send your next mailing. By this time, your website should be complete and your mouse pads should have arrived. This is an easy mailing, as you are sending nothing but the mouse pad in the colored plastic envelope. Stuff one mouse pad into each envelope, label, and send. Your web designer should have a way to track the number of hits your website receives. Watch the number of people who visit your website after this mailing. The phone might start ringing, too.

To market yourself successfully, you must be able to relate to your clients. The initial image you portray is critical to attracting your target demographic. Be sure you understand who it is you're trying to relate to. Think about what sort of image will make your target clients feel comfortable with your representation. Remember, you are not trying to recreate a company image or your own major brand or logo, but rather to integrate your company's colors, logo, image, and perception with your individuality and expertise. I would never try to outdo my company's presence with my own image. Your company has already spent thousands (or millions) of dollars imprinting its image on the community, and has more than likely hired professional advertising companies and graphic designers to design an image to which people respond. Use this to your advantage by co-branding yourself with that image. Dr. Joyce Brothers said it best: "A strong, positive self-image is the best possible preparation for success in life."

Through your marketing efforts, a subtle change in conversations and face recognition will take place over time. As you go on caravan, into shops, or out with your friends, it is likely that people will start talking to you about real estate. If you've been reaching a wide audience with your photo, they might start recognizing your efforts and comment on seeing you "everywhere." This is great feedback. Keep up the effort.

Public Relations

One of the best ways to gain free publicity is through public relations. There is a saying: "Everything you do or say is public relations." Do not take this lightly. PR can be an extremely powerful tool. Not only is PR often free, but it is one of the most effective methods of persuasion. Essentially, PR is a third party vouching for your credibility or creating awareness about your brand. It is usually seen in the form of an article or interview. PR mediums are not always frequent and easy to come by, as they require newsworthy information and networking. These opportunities often have to be sought out and require prudent timing.

I was very fortunate to have received the amount of PR that I did in the beginning of my career. I was quoted on Forbes.com the same week that I was interviewed to be on Bravo's *Million Dollar Listing*. The Forbes.com opportunity came from the manager of the hotel where I had worked previously. A Forbes.com representative called the hotel to acquire information about real estate in Malibu. The manager didn't feel comfortable being quoted about an industry he did not specialize in, so he referred the interviewer to me. As far as Bravo is concerned, I received a call from a producer who wanted to interview me for possible casting in a new reality documentary show. The channel had found my information through a local real estate magazine, where I was advertising my three listings. One thing led to the next, and we were filming before I knew it. Both of these incidents had a lot to do with being in the right place at the right time, but that doesn't mean that all public relations efforts are strictly serendipitous. Some PR efforts are created by you.

As mentioned earlier in this chapter, you need to ask your manager or office administrator to post an announcement in the local newspapers regarding your new position with the company. This is the easiest way to gain recognition in your community. Another inexpensive way to promote your image is through the Internet. Social media websites like Facebook, Twitter, Instagram, and YouTube allow you to post or blog information at no cost. Social channels give you creative freedom and the ability to share valuable information with current and potential clients. You can post pictures of new listings and showcase properties you've successfully sold or leased. When your clients and prospects see your success, they will begin to envision how you can help them, as well.

While it's unlikely that someone will hire you strictly based on your social media presence, it's amazing how it will contribute to the buzz you're creating for yourself. The more often people see your name, the more likely it is that your name will become associated with your profession. You are trying to build your presence in order to persuade your contacts to refer business to you.

The announcement letter and follow-up email highlighted earlier are also powerful PR tools. Keep in mind that your announcement letter should not request recipients' personal business, but rather inform them that you have begun a new career and provide them with your contact information. Be sure to literally ask how you can be of assistance to them and their business. In the months to come, if you have a newsworthy accomplishment related to your business, send an email thanking everyone for their support (whether or not they had anything to do with it). I've received many referrals using this technique without ever asking for them.

The phone rang. It was the director of my company's training program. "Hey," he said, "you wanna come talk to the newbies *again?*"

I thought, "I ought to write a book."

CHAPTER 13

It Is *Your* Time

It is my hope that this book will help you recognize your passion, activate it, and structure a successful career around it. I attribute my success to many things, but the most important factor is passion. The passion I have for people is suited perfectly to my career in real estate. Developing my passion into a successful career required me to find the positive in all situations. By staying focused on the people, I have been able to seize opportunities in unexpected places. I have been able to build success upon a foundation that some might have perceived as deeply flawed. All the while, I have continued the journey that began in my childhood, with each new move. Every new home was an opportunity to connect with people.

Using the tools in this book is not about repeating a simple slogan and hoping for a miracle. It is a practice, a meditation, an awareness of how you interpret situations, and how you listen to your instincts. From the moment I committed myself to this career, I saw nothing but opportunity. I stepped away from my fears and saw no other alternative but to succeed. I learned that fear is overcome by committing to success versus failure. This takes work. I did not allow my location, the competition, market trends, negativity from my peers or colleagues, or my young age to deter me from committing to success. I didn't even allow the word "failure" into my vocabulary. Stay focused on the goals you've set for yourself and reinforce your commitment to attain them.

Remain ethical and positive. Even during the worst of times, find the positive and focus on that. Work hard. Have fun with your passion, stop and smell the roses along the way, and don't forget to enjoy the fruits of your labors and reward yourself for any progress. Acknowledging progress creates a feeling of well-being; that pause simply to feel good will encourage your mind and body to seek and attain the next goal. Stay healthy and fit, remain balanced and determined, and be prepared to succeed!

Your passion, once you find it and recognize it, is a blessing. It is a guiding beacon. It is a gift. If you have trouble recognizing it as a gift, don't worry. I know a woman who will wrap it for you brilliantly. I believe she's charging for that service now, but she's worth every penny. And she's very good at what she does.

GLOSSARY OF TERMS

Addendum: An addition or change to a contract.

Bullpen: An office area where many employees share an open workspace.

Caravan: A decided weekday when real estate agents have the opportunity to have their listings open for viewings by other agents. It is an opportunity for real estate agents to preview available properties and familiarize themselves with the inventory.

Commission: The negotiable percentage of the sales price of a property that is paid to the agents of the buyer and seller.

Commission split: The division of the payment made to the listing agent between that agent and her broker, or between the listing agent and the agent representing the purchaser.

Contract: An agreement between two or more parties that creates or modifies an existing relationship.

Disclosure: A statement to a potential buyer listing information relevant to a piece of property, such as the presence of radon or lead paint.

Dual agency: When a real estate agent represents both the seller and the buyer in the transaction on the subject property.

Escrow: A neutral third party which holds the documents and money involved in a real estate transaction and ensures that all conditions of a sale are met. Escrow also refers to an account that a lender establishes to hold monthly installments from the borrower to cover property taxes and insurance.

Fiduciary duty: The relationship of trust that buyers and sellers expect from a real estate agent. The term also applies to legal and business relationships.

Flipping: Buying property and reselling it quickly for a profit.

Interest rate: The sum, expressed as a percentage, charged for a loan. Interest payments on most home loans are tax deductible.

Lender: A bank, savings institution, or mortgage company that offers home loans.

Market share: The percentage of the total sales of a given type of product or service that is attributable to a given company.

Title: The actual legal document conferring ownership of a piece of real estate.

Top producer: A real estate industry term that refers to agents and brokers who sell a high volume of homes.

ABOUT THE AUTHOR

Madison Hildebrand, President and Founder of The Malibu Life, Inc., is one of the most recognizable faces in the world of real estate. As an esteemed and respected luxury real estate agent, Madison is a consummate professional and negotiating expert, with over $250 million in career sales.

After completing his Bachelor of Arts in Advertising from Pepperdine University, Madison became a pillar within the Malibu community. He serves as a current Board Member of the Malibu Boys and Girls Club, a past Board Director of the Malibu Association of Realtors, a weekly volunteer at the ER at the UCLA Santa Monica Hospital, and Vice President of The Malibu Green Machine.

A six-year veteran of the small screen, Madison is most widely known as the original cast member of Bravo's popular television series *Million Dollar Listing Los Angeles* and as a contributing host on *E! News*. His most recent accomplishments include signing on as Brand Ambassador for the eSignature company, DocuSign, as well as producing a national seminar tour where he coaches realtors across the country on creating their own personal and professional blueprint for success. Whether it's gardening, traveling, or hiking with his rescue Doberman, Maya, Madison lives by his philosophy, "You *can* mix business with pleasure."

INDEX

Made in the USA
San Bernardino, CA
09 October 2017